Real Food
from your
Casserole

Jean Conil

foulsham
LONDON • NEW YORK • TORONTO • SYDNEY

foulsham

The Publishing House, Bennetts Close,
Cippenham, Berks, SL1 5AP, England

ISBN 0-572-02671-4

Originally published as *Quick & Easy One-pot Casseroles.*

Printed in Great Britain by The Bath Press, Bath

CONTENTS

ABOUT THE AUTHOR

Jean Conil was trained in Paris and inspired by Escoffier, whom he met in 1932. He worked in the south of France and on board luxury French liners in the days before the Second World War. He has become well-known in Britain for his articles on cookery in *The Sunday Times* and in magazines. He is the author of more than 100 cookery books including the best-sellers: *French Home Cookery, Haute Cuisine* and *Cuisine Vegetarienne Française.*

Jean Conil was the executive chef and catering manager of Fortnum and Mason, the Hurlingham Club, the Arts Club and the Athenaeum Hotel in Park Lane. He is the founder and life administrative president of the prestigious Epicurean World Master Chefs' Society.

INTRODUCTION

The word 'casserole' is used to describe a lidded vessel in which the ingredients are cooked slowly, usually in a preheated oven. By extension, the name 'casserole' is also applied to the dishes cooked in such containers. The wonderful thing about casseroles is that they are very quick to prepare and can be left to cook gently with the minimum of attention, so nothing could be easier. The other great advantage is you can use inexpensive cuts of meat and still create tender and delicious dishes. The same pot can be used for the preparation, cooking and serving of the dish, so there's very little washing-up either!

Choose a flameproof casserole (Dutch oven) made of cast iron, stainless steel, copper, ceramic or earthenware with a heavy base which can be used on top of the cooker when ingredients need to be precooked before being put into the oven. Look for the word 'flameproof' on the label. If the dish is only 'ovenproof' it cannot be used on direct heat.

Enamelled cast iron is regarded as one of the best materials for cookware. It enhances the flavour of any food cooked in it, whether by slow cooking in the oven, or boiling, or frying (sautéing) on the hob. It also maintains a more even heat, which it holds for longer than other cookware materials. Use only nylon pads to clean the pot and avoid harsh abrasive cleaners or wire pads. Do not heat over 230°C/450°F/gas mark 8 when using lids with plastic knobs, and remember to use protective oven gloves when handling casseroles that do not have insulated or wooden handles.

Many dishes in this book are meals in themselves; others need only some crusty bread, a fresh vegetable, rice or a green salad. Alternatively, pop some jacket potatoes or a smaller casserole dish containing diced root vegetables in the oven at the same time.

All the recipes can easily be adapted for cooking in a slo-cooker.

NOTES ON THE RECIPES

◇ Ingredients are given in metric, imperial and American measures. Use only one set per recipe, don't interchange.

◇ All spoon measures are level: 1 tsp = 5 ml
                                  1 tbsp = 15 ml

◇ Eggs are medium unless otherwise stated.

◇ All herbs are fresh unless otherwise stated. To substitute dried, use only half the quantity as they are very pungent.

◇ Wash, dry and peel, if necessary, fresh produce before using.

◇ Preparation and cooking times given at the end of each recipe are approximate and should be used as a guide only. In particular, you may need to reduce cooking times or temperatures when using a fan-assisted oven.

◇ Make sure the casserole dish you use is the correct size to hold the ingredients comfortably. If it is over-full, the food will take longer to cook. If the dish is too large, the ingredients may dry out.

◇ To make seasoned flour, add 2.5 ml/½ tsp of salt and a good pinch of freshly ground black pepper to 50 g/2 oz/½ cup of plain (all-purpose) flour.

COUNTRY CASSEROLE SOUPS

For centuries, peasant soups were produced from a black pot suspended over the fire in farm households. These hot-pot soups were covered with a lid and the contents – meat and vegetables – simmered gently for hours until the ingredients, enhanced by herbs, produced a wonderfully concentrated flavour with barely any effort at all. These delicious soups were meals in themselves and many of these delicious recipes survive today.

All soups can be fortified with meat or yeast extracts, or stock cubes dissolved in water. Extra garnishes that complement the ingredients, such as croûtons, cooked rice or vermicelli, can be added for extra sustenance. Country soups made with pulses and beans are extremely nourishing and provide a wholesome and varied diet. For a richer flavour, fry (sauté) the meat and vegetables first.

KING LOUIS' CONSOMMÉ

It is said that the French king Louis XVI frequently over-ate and needed tonic broths to settle his system. He considered this concentrated beef-tea to be the best medicine.

—— SERVES 4 ——

	METRIC	IMPERIAL	AMERICAN
Lean minced (ground) beef	450 g	1 lb	2 cups
Raw beetroot (red beet), peeled and grated	50 g	2 oz	½ cup
Onion, chopped	25 g	1 oz	¼ cup
Carrot, grated	50 g	2 oz	½ cup
Fennel, grated	25 g	1 oz	¼ cup
Egg white	1	1	1
Salt and freshly ground black pepper			
White port	150 ml	¼ pt	⅔ cup

① Combine all the ingredients in a casserole (Dutch oven) and leave to soak for 1 hour.

② Cover and braise in a preheated oven at 180°C/350°F/gas mark 4 for 2 hours. The solids will gradually come to the top and form a thick crust during cooking and the liquid will be clear, limpid and aromatic.

③ To serve the consommé, simply make a small hole in the crust, ensuring that the rest remains unbroken, and pour off the liquor. Alternatively, you can strain the consommé through a muslin cloth (cheesecloth). Discard the solids completely.

PREPARATION TIME: 10 MINUTES PLUS SOAKING

COOKING TIME: 2 HOURS

CASSOULET SOUP

This soup is made with goose or duck legs cooked in plenty of liquid with haricot (navy) beans and tomatoes until the meat is completely separated from the bones and the beans are soft enough to be puréed into a thick soup. You can use chicken or turkey if you prefer.

—— SERVES 4 ——

	METRIC	IMPERIAL	AMERICAN
Duck or goose drumsticks	2	2	2
Oil	30 ml	2 tbsp	2 tbsp
Haricot beans, soaked overnight in cold water	100 g	4 oz	1 cup
Onion, sliced	1	1	1
Carrot, sliced	1	1	1
Onion, chopped	1	1	1
Garlic cloves, crushed	2	2	2
Salt and freshly ground black pepper			
Water	600 ml	1 pt	2½ cups
White wine	600 ml	1 pt	2½ cups
French bread, to serve			

① Put all the ingredients in a metal casserole (Dutch oven).

② Cover and braise in a preheated oven at 180°C/350°F/gas mark 4 for 2 hours.

③ Remove from the oven and lift out any bones. Liquidise the soup to a thin purée.

④ Serve with French bread.

PREPARATION TIME: 5 MINUTES PLUS SOAKING
COOKING TIME: 2 HOURS

LEEK AND CHICKEN SOUP

Delicious, tasty poultry soups can be produced in casserole dishes (Dutch ovens) using only wings and giblets. This recipe has been in my family for years. The delicate aroma of leeks enhances the natural flavour of chicken and using the skin from the chicken gives the soup more flavour.

—— SERVES 4 ——

	METRIC	IMPERIAL	AMERICAN
Butter or margarine	50 g	2 oz	¼ cup
Chicken wings and mixed giblets	1 kg	2¼ lb	2¼ lb
Leeks, sliced	2	2	2
Potatoes, finely diced	150 g	5 oz	5 oz
Salt and freshly ground black pepper			
Water	1.2 litres	2 pts	5 cups
Chicken stock cubes, crumbled	2	2	2
Double (heavy) cream (optional)	150 ml	¼ pt	⅔ cup

① Melt the butter or margarine in a flameproof casserole and fry (sauté) the chicken wings and giblets for 5 minutes until browned.

② Add the leeks and potatoes and season to taste with salt and pepper. Add the water and stock cubes and bring to the boil.

③ Cover and cook in a preheated oven at 180°C/350°F/gas mark 4 for 1½ hours until tender.

④ Strain the soup to remove the bones, then return the meat and vegetables to the pan.

⑤ For a richer soup, spoon in some double cream before serving, or serve it separately for your guests to help themselves.

PREPARATION TIME: 10 MINUTES
COOKING TIME: 1½ HOURS

THICK PEA SOUP

Split peas are at their best when cooked in casseroles (Dutch ovens), where they make a hearty, thick soup. Always popular, this well-known English soup is made more interesting when cooked with unsmoked bacon.

—— SERVES 4 ——

	METRIC	IMPERIAL	AMERICAN
Split peas, soaked in cold water for 2 hours	150 g	5 oz	⅔ cup
Onion, chopped	1	1	1
Celery stick, chopped	1	1	1
Spinach leaves, shredded	6	6	6
Back bacon, rinded and diced	150 g	5 oz	5 oz
Water	1.3 litres	2¼ pts	5½ cups
For the croûtons:			
Bread slices, crusts removed and cut into squares	4	4	4
Olive oil			

① Put all the main ingredients in a metal casserole and braise slowly in a preheated oven at 180°C/350°F/gas mark 4 for 1½ hours.

② Strain the soup or liquidise to a thin purée.

③ To make the croûtons, sprinkle the bread liberally with olive oil and toss well. Bake in a preheated oven at 200°C/400°F/gas mark 6 for about 10 minutes, stirring occasionally, until crisp and golden.

④ Serve the soup with the croûtons offered separately.

PREPARATION TIME: 10 MINUTES PLUS SOAKING
COOKING TIME: 1½ HOURS

CANADIAN COD CHOWDER

The word 'chowder' is derived from the old French word *chaudron,* a cast iron cooking pot, although it is more usually applied to a casserole of fresh or salted cod.

—— SERVES 4 ——

	METRIC	IMPERIAL	AMERICAN
Cod, skinned, boned and diced	1 kg	2¼ lb	2¼ lb
Onion, chopped	1	1	1
Carrot, chopped	1	1	1
Celery stick, chopped	1	1	1
Dried thyme	5 ml	1 tsp	1 tsp
Potato, diced	225 g	8 oz	2 cups
Fresh basil leaves, chopped	3	3	3
Butter or margarine	50 g	2 oz	¼ cup
Fish stock or water	1.3 litres	2¼ pts	5½ cups
Salt and freshly ground black pepper			
Fresh crusty bread, to serve			

① Layer all the ingredients in a casserole (Dutch oven), dotting with butter or margarine as you go. Cover with the stock or water and season with salt and pepper.

② Cover and braise gently in a preheated oven at 180°C/350°F/gas mark 4 for 1 hour.

③ Serve in warmed soup bowls with fresh crusty bread.

PREPARATION TIME: 10 MINUTES
COOKING TIME: 1 HOUR

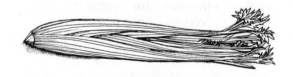

AFRICAN LAMB SOUP WITH COUSCOUS

Lamb is extremely popular all over northern Africa, and most countries in the region produce their own version of this thick, soup-style casserole. It is the pungency of the herbs and spices – fennel, saffron, cumin, garlic and chilli – that give the couscous soup its distinctive and wholesome character.

—— SERVES 6 ——

	METRIC	IMPERIAL	AMERICAN
Lean shoulder or neck of lamb, diced	225 g	8 oz	2 cups
Fennel bulb, diced	I	I	I
Carrot, diced	I	I	I
Celery stick, sliced	I	I	I
Courgette (zucchini), sliced	I	I	I
Green chilli, sliced	I	I	I
Onion, sliced	I	I	I
Garlic cloves, chopped	2	2	2
A pinch of cumin seed			
A pinch of saffron powder			
Water	1.3 litres	2¼ pts	5½ cups
Couscous	50 g	2 oz	⅓ cup
Butter or margarine, melted	25 g	I oz	2 tbsp

① Put all the ingredients, except the couscous and melted butter or margarine, in a casserole (Dutch oven) and braise gently in a preheated oven at 180°C/350°F/gas mark 4 for 1¾ hours.

② Combine the couscous with the melted butter or margarine and stir it into the hot soup. Cook for a further 10 minutes to heat through before serving.

PREPARATION TIME: 15 MINUTES
COOKING TIME: 2 HOURS

KING HENRY'S HOT-POT SOUP

Henry IV, King of Navarre and France, was the first monarch to take an interest in agriculture, recognising the need for more and better food for the impoverished French people. 'I want everyone in France,' he said, 'to be able to afford a chicken in the soup pot once a week.' At that time the diet of the ordinary workers was meagre and largely vegetarian.

—— SERVES 6 ——

	METRIC	IMPERIAL	AMERICAN
Small oven-ready chicken	1	1	1
Leeks, sliced	2	2	2
Carrots, sliced	2	2	2
Turnip, diced	1	1	1
Celery stick, diced	1	1	1
A sprig of thyme			
Water	1.75 litres	3 pts	7½ cups
Salt	5 ml	1 tsp	1 tsp
Black peppercorns, crushed	6	6	6

① Put all the ingredients in a casserole (Dutch oven), cover and braise gently in a preheated oven at 180°C/350°F/gas mark 4 for 1¼ hours until the chicken is tender.

② Remove the chicken from the broth. Either carve the chicken into portions and serve it with the vegetables and broth, or liquidise the vegetables in the stock for a thick soup and serve the chicken separately as a main course.

PREPARATION TIME: 5 MINUTES
COOKING TIME: 1¼ HOURS

SEAFOOD CASSEROLES

Many classic seafood dishes are baked in casseroles (Dutch ovens) and this method makes the most delicious dishes out of ordinary and very inexpensive fish. I have selected the most tasty recipes that are simple to prepare and quick to cook. Some include fish and rice combinations, which work very well, while large pieces of fish on the bone are particularly good when cooked with sliced potatoes.

When buying fish, look for signs of quality and freshness: shining skin, pink gills and full, bright eyes with black pupils and transparent corneas. The flesh should be firm and springy. Fresh fish should have a clean, pleasant odour. Choose fish with translucent, rather than milky, flesh. Fillets that are dried up around the edges and show traces of discoloration will be stale.

If you buy fish whole, gut them as soon as possible as the digestive organs contain powerful enzymes that will attack the body wall. The only ones that can be kept intact for any length of time are fish such as salmon and sea trout, because during the breeding season, when they are caught, the digestive organs of these fish waste away.

Seafood will not keep for more than a day or two in a fridge and should be loosely wrapped in clingfilm (plastic wrap) or foil to prevent the smell from spreading and contaminating other foods. All fish should be washed in salt water with a little vinegar (15 ml/1 tbsp per 600 ml/1 pt/2½ cups) before cooking.

Most fish taste best when marinated or cooked in water or oils flavoured with herbs. A fresh herring or mackerel, however, requires nothing more than a knob of butter and a squeeze of lemon juice.

COD CASSEROLE WITH CHEESE

The curry powder in this recipe adds piquancy to the fish.

—— SERVES 4 ——

	METRIC	IMPERIAL	AMERICAN
Seasoned plain (all-purpose) flour	60 ml	4 tbsp	4 tbsp
Curry powder	5 ml	I tsp	I tsp
Cod fillet, skinned and cut into 4 portions	I kg	2¼ lb	2¼ lb
Butter or margarine, melted	40 g	1½ oz	3 tbsp
Shallot, chopped	I	I	I
Mushrooms, sliced	4	4	4
Salt and white pepper			
Dry white wine	75 ml	5 tbsp	5 tbsp
Chopped fresh thyme	5 ml	I tsp	I tsp
Fish stock cube	I	I	I
Hot water	75 ml	5 tbsp	5 tbsp
Cheddar cheese, grated	50 g	2 oz	½ cup
Double (heavy) cream	60 ml	4 tbsp	4 tbsp
Chopped fresh parsley	45 ml	3 tbsp	3 tbsp
Crusty bread, to serve			

① Combine the seasoned flour with the curry powder and use to coat the cod fillets.

② Pour the melted butter or margarine into a casserole (Dutch oven), sprinkle the shallot and mushrooms over and lay the fish fillets on top. Season to taste with salt and pepper. Add the wine and thyme. Dissolve the stock cube in the hot water and pour over the casserole. Sprinkle over the grated cheese.

③ Cover and cook in a preheated oven at 200°C/400°F/gas mark 6 for 20 minutes.

④ When ready to serve, stir the cream into the fish liquor, sprinkle over the parsley and serve with crusty bread.

PREPARATION TIME: 10 MINUTES

COOKING TIME: 20 MINUTES

IDEAL WITH MUSCADET, CHABLIS OR DRY CIDER

TUNA PROVENÇALE

In an emergency you could use canned tuna for this recipe. The dish can be served hot or cold.

—— SERVES 6 ——

	METRIC	IMPERIAL	AMERICAN
Fresh tuna, cut into 2.5 cm/1 in cubes	1 kg	2¼ lb	2¼ lb
Onion, chopped	1	1	1
Olive oil	45 ml	3 tbsp	3 tbsp
Aubergine (eggplant), peeled and cut into 2.5 cm/1 in cubes	1	1	1
Large tomato, skinned, seeded and chopped	1	1	1
Black olives, stoned (pitted)	8	8	8
Garlic cloves, chopped	2	2	2
A few fresh basil leaves, chopped			
Water or fish stock	300 ml	½ pt	1¼ cups
Salt and freshly ground black pepper			
Boiled rice or a green salad, to serve			

1. Place the tuna in a casserole (Dutch oven) and add the onion, oil, aubergine, tomato, black olives, garlic and basil. Add the water or fish stock and season with a little salt and a good pinch of black pepper.

2. Cover and cook in a preheated oven at 200°C/400°F/gas mark 6 for 20 minutes.

3. Serve hot with boiled rice or cold with green salad.

PREPARATION TIME: 20 MINUTES
COOKING TIME: 20 MINUTES
LIGHT ROSÉ WINE OR DRY CIDER MAKE GOOD ACCOMPANIMENTS

SCANDINAVIAN FISH DUMPLINGS

These light dumplings make an excellent buffet party dish.

—— SERVES 4–6 ——

	METRIC	IMPERIAL	AMERICAN
Cod fillet, skinned	I kg	2¼ lb	2¼ lb
Onion, finely chopped	I	I	I
Fresh white breadcrumbs	30 ml	2 tbsp	2 tbsp
Caster (superfine) sugar	5 ml	I tsp	I tsp
Egg	I	I	I
Salt	5 ml	I tsp	I tsp
A pinch of white pepper			
Carrot, diagonally sliced	I	I	I
Onion, sliced	I	I	I
Fish stock or water	600 ml	I pt	2½ cups
Juice of I lemon			
A sprig of fennel or dill (dill weed)			
Sliced beetroot (red beet) and celery salad, or mangetout (snow peas), to serve			

① Mince (grind) the fish, then blend it with the chopped onion, breadcrumbs, sugar, egg, salt and white pepper. Divide the mixture into 50 g/2 oz dumplings (it will make about 18).

② Half-fill a casserole (Dutch oven) with the carrot and sliced onion. Add the fish stock or water. Place the dumplings in the dish. Sprinkle with the lemon juice and add the fennel or dill. Season to taste with salt and pepper.

③ Cover and cook in a preheated oven at 200°C/400°F/gas mark 6 for 20 minutes.

④ Serve hot or cold with sliced beetroot and celery salad or with mangetout.

PREPARATION TIME: 20 MINUTES

COOKING TIME: 20 MINUTES

HOCK, ALSACE OR SPARKLING WHITE WINE TO ACCOMPANY

SWEDISH-STYLE SMOKED HERRING CASSEROLE

If you can't find salted smoked herring, use kipper fillets.

—— SERVES 4 ——

	METRIC	IMPERIAL	AMERICAN
Salted smoked herring fillets, about 50 g/2 oz each	8	8	8
Potatoes, thinly sliced	450 g	1 lb	1 lb
Onion, sliced	1	1	1
Juice of 1 lemon			
Single (light) cream	300 ml	½ pt	1¼ cups
Fresh dill (dill weed), coarsely chopped	15 ml	1 tbsp	1 tbsp
Salt and freshly ground black pepper			

① Wash the herring fillets under cold running water for 15 minutes to remove the excess salt. Drain and pat dry.

② Blanch the sliced potatoes for 2 minutes in boiling water, then drain.

③ Place a layer of half the potatoes and onion in a casserole (Dutch oven) and cover with the herring. Mix together the lemon juice and cream and pour half the mixture over the fish. Cover with the remaining potatoes and onions and the dill, then pour over the remaining cream and season to taste with salt and pepper.

④ Cover and bake in a preheated oven at 180°C/350°F/gas mark 4 for 30 minutes.

PREPARATION TIME: 20 MINUTES
COOKING TIME: 30 MINUTES
WHITE BURGUNDY OR LIGHT ROSÉ WINE TO ACCOMPANY

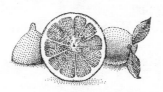

SALMON CASSEROLE WITH BASMATI RICE

Basmati rice has a delicate texture, flavour and aroma. The word *basmati* actually means 'the fragrant one'. Easy-cook basmati is pre-steamed to seal in the goodness, and guaranteed to produce fluffy, separate grains every time.

—— SERVES 3–4 ——

	METRIC	IMPERIAL	AMERICAN
Basmati rice	100 g	4 oz	½ cup
Butter or margarine, melted	50 g	2 oz	¼ cup
Salmon, skinned and cut into small pieces	225 g	8 oz	8 oz
Shallot, chopped	1	1	1
A sprig of dill (dill weed), chopped			
Juice of 1 lemon			
Grated rind of ½ lemon			
Water	300 ml	½ pt	1¼ cups
Salt and freshly ground black pepper			
Cucumber salad with yoghurt and chopped fresh mint, to serve			

① Combine the rice and melted butter or margarine in a casserole (Dutch oven), then stir in the fish, shallot, dill, lemon juice and grated lemon rind. Pour in the water and season with salt and pepper.

② Cover and bake in a preheated oven at 200°C/400°F/gas mark 6 for 20–25 minutes.

③ Serve with a cucumber salad blended with yoghurt and chopped fresh mint.

PREPARATION TIME: 10 MINUTES
COOKING TIME: 20–25 MINUTES
LIME CORDIAL AND SODA WATER TO ACCOMPANY

FILLET OF SOLE WITH GRAPES

This classic dish is equally good made with plaice fillets.

—— SERVES 2 ——

	METRIC	IMPERIAL	AMERICAN
Sole fillets, about 75 g/3 oz each	4	4	4
Seasoned plain (all-purpose) flour	15 ml	1 tbsp	1 tbsp
Butter or margarine, melted	50 g	2 oz	¼ cup
Shallot, chopped	1	1	1
Dry white wine	150 ml	¼ pt	¾ cup
Salt and freshly ground black pepper			
Seedless grapes	150 g	5 oz	5 oz
Double (heavy) cream	120 ml	4 fl oz	½ cup

① Gently beat the sole fillets with a wooden mallet to prevent curling during cooking.

② Coat the fillets in the seasoned flour, shaking off the surplus.

③ Put the melted butter or margarine and chopped shallot into a casserole (Dutch oven). Lay the sole fillets over the mixture and cover with white wine. Season to taste with salt and pepper. Sprinkle the grapes on top.

④ Cover and bake in a preheated oven at 200°C/400°F/gas mark 6 for 15–20 minutes.

⑤ Blend the cream into the fish liquor. Check the seasoning and serve from the dish.

PREPARATION TIME: 10 MINUTES
COOKING TIME: 15–20 MINUTES
SANCERRE, MUSCADET OR ANJOU WINE TO ACCOMPANY

GREEK MACKEREL CASSEROLE

—— SERVES 4 AS A STARTER ——

	METRIC	IMPERIAL	AMERICAN
Mackerel fillets, cut into small pieces	4	4	4
Dry white wine	300 ml	½ pt	1¼ cups
Olive oil	45 ml	3 tbsp	3 tbsp
Spring onions (scallions), chopped	150 g	5 oz	5 oz
Button mushrooms	150 g	5 oz	5 oz
Fennel stalk, cut into small strips	1	1	1
Salt			
Black peppercorns, crushed	5 ml	1 tsp	1 tsp
Chopped fresh parsley	30 ml	2 tbsp	2 tbsp

① Place the fish pieces in a casserole (Dutch oven) with all the ingredients except the parsley.

② Cover and bake in a preheated oven at 200°C/400°F/gas mark 6 for 25 minutes.

③ Leave to cool to room temperature, then serve with a sprinkling of parsley.

PREPARATION TIME: 10 MINUTES

COOKING TIME: 25 MINUTES

WHITE BORDEAUX OR MACON TO ACCOMPANY

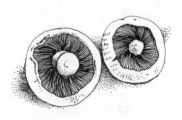

PRAWN-STUFFED MARROW BOATS

This mixture makes a delicious stuffing for courgettes (zucchini) too.

—— SERVES 4 AS A HOT STARTER ——

	METRIC	IMPERIAL	AMERICAN
Young marrow (squash), peeled	I	I	I
Peeled prawns (shrimp)	450 g	I lb	I lb
Shallot, chopped	I	I	I
Carrot, grated	150 g	5 oz	1¼ cups
Chopped fresh mint	5 ml	I tsp	I tsp
Soured (dairy sour) cream	120 ml	4 fl oz	½ cup
Salt and freshly ground black pepper			
Curry powder	5 ml	I tsp	I tsp
Paprika	5 ml	I tsp	I tsp
Strong cheese, grated	100 g	4 oz	I cup

① Cut the marrow in half lengthways. Remove the seeds with a spoon to form a cavity. Divide the marrow into four pieces and boil in salted water in a flameproof casserole (Dutch oven) for no more than 6 minutes. Drain and return to the casserole, hollow side up.

② Combine the prawns with the shallot, carrots, mint and soured cream. Season with salt, pepper, curry powder and paprika.

③ Fill the marrow boats with the prawn mixture and sprinkle over the grated cheese.

④ Bake, uncovered, in a preheated oven at 200°C/400°F/gas mark 6 for 15 minutes until golden brown.

PREPARATION TIME: 15 MINUTES
COOKING TIME: 15 MINUTES
HOCK OR OTHER LIGHT, FRUITY GERMAN WINE TO ACCOMPANY

HALIBUT FILLETS ON A BED OF SPINACH

This delicate, oily fish goes very well with spinach. In order to preserve the precious minerals and flavour, it is best to cook spinach without water.

—— SERVES 2–4 ——

	METRIC	IMPERIAL	AMERICAN
Fresh spinach	450 g	1 lb	1 lb
Thick Greek yoghurt	150 ml	¼ pt	¾ cup
Halibut fillets, about 225 g/8 oz each	4	4	4
Salt and freshly ground black pepper			
A good pinch of grated nutmeg			
Garlic cloves, chopped	2	2	2
Water	120 ml	4 fl oz	½ cup
Flaked (slivered) peanuts, toasted	30 ml	2 tbsp	2 tbsp
Boiled new potatoes or plain boiled rice, to serve			

① Wash the spinach in plenty of water. Drain and pat dry with a clean cloth. Gently squeeze out any surplus water.

② Place the spinach in a deep casserole (Dutch oven).

③ Spread a thick coating of yoghurt over the fish fillets. Season to taste with salt, pepper and nutmeg. Arrange the fillets on top of the spinach leaves and press down a little.

④ Liquidise the garlic with the water and pour over the fish, then sprinkle the peanuts over the top.

⑤ Cover and bake in a preheated oven at 200°C/400°F/gas mark 6 for 20 minutes.

⑥ Serve with boiled new potatoes or plain boiled rice.

PREPARATION TIME: 15 MINUTES
COOKING TIME: 20 MINUTES
CHARDONNAY TO ACCOMPANY

INDIAN-STYLE FISH CASSEROLE

Nowadays, some fish is more expensive than meat. However, the rice in this recipe helps a little to go a long way.

—— SERVES 4 ——

	METRIC	IMPERIAL	AMERICAN
Mild curry powder	30 ml	2 tbsp	2 tbsp
Plain (all-purpose) flour	30 ml	2 tbsp	2 tbsp
Garlic cloves, chopped	2	2	2
Green chilli, chopped	1	1	1
Haddock or pollack fillets, unskinned, about 225 g/8 oz each	4	4	4
Soya oil	60 ml	4 tbsp	4 tbsp
Bananas, peeled and sliced diagonally	6	6	6
Large tomatoes, skinned, seeded and chopped	6	6	6
Desiccated (shredded) coconut	15 ml	1 tbsp	1 tbsp
Chopped fresh coriander (cilantro) or parsley	30 ml	2 tbsp	2 tbsp

① Mix together the curry powder, flour, garlic and chilli and use the mixture to coat the fish fillets.

② Heat the oil in a flameproof casserole (Dutch oven) and fry (sauté) the fish on one side only for 4 minutes.

③ Place the sliced banana and chopped tomatoes in the casserole on top of the fish. Sprinkle over the desiccated coconut.

④ Cover and cook in a preheated oven at 220°C/425°F/gas mark 7 for 12 minutes.

⑤ Sprinkle over the chopped coriander or parsley just before serving.

PREPARATION TIME: 15 MINUTES
COOKING TIME: 12 MINUTES
CHILLED LAGER TO ACCOMPANY

HAKE HOT-POT

Use a heavy casserole (Dutch oven) for this recipe. Hake is probably one of the tastiest white fish we can eat. It can be prepared in the same way as cod but has firmer flesh and is delicious served cold with mayonnaise.

—— SERVES 4–6 ——

	METRIC	IMPERIAL	AMERICAN
Peanut (groundnut) oil	60 ml	4 tbsp	4 tbsp
Onions, chopped	2	2	2
Celery stick, chopped	I	I	I
Fennel bulb, chopped	I	I	I
New potatoes, sliced	450 g	I lb	I lb
Water	I litre	I¾ pts	4¼ cups
A sprig of thyme			
Salt	5 ml	I tsp	I tsp
Freshly ground black pepper	5 ml	I tsp	I tsp
Hake fillets, skinned and cut into 4–6 portions	I kg	2¼ lb	2¼ lb
Tomatoes, skinned, seeded and chopped	4	4	4
Chopped fresh parsley	45 ml	3 tbsp	3 tbsp

① Heat the oil in a flameproof casserole and fry (sauté) the onions, celery and fennel for 4 minutes.

② Add the potatoes, water and thyme and season with salt and pepper.

③ Bake in a preheated oven at 200°C/400°F/gas mark 6 for 15 minutes.

④ Remove the casserole from the oven, place the fish on top of the vegetables and cover with the chopped tomatoes. Cover and bake for a further 8 minutes. Serve from the pot with a good sprinkling of parsley.

PREPARATION TIME: 20 MINUTES
COOKING TIME: 23 MINUTES
LIGHTLY SPARKLING PORTUGUESE ROSÉ TO ACCOMPANY

SALMON STEAKS IN MUSTARD SAUCE

Extensive salmon farming means that salmon is now almost as cheap as cod, and it is certainly as versatile. As the central bone and skin are easily removed once cooked and they contribute to the flavour, I suggest they are left in during cooking.

—— SERVES 4 ——

	METRIC	IMPERIAL	AMERICAN
Butter or margarine	50 g	2 oz	¼ cup
Garlic cloves, chopped	2	2	2
Shallots, chopped	8	8	8
Salmon steaks, about 225 g/ 8 oz each	4	4	4
Juice of 1 lemon			
Mild mustard	45 ml	3 tbsp	3 tbsp
Single (light) cream	300 ml	½ pt	1¼ cups
Salt and freshly ground black pepper			
Chopped fresh basil, mint and parsley, mixed	30 ml	2 tbsp	2 tbsp
Chopped fresh dill (dill weed)	45 ml	3 tbsp	3 tbsp
Cucumber salad, to serve			

① Grease a large casserole (Dutch oven) or four individual gratin dishes with butter or margarine. Sprinkle in the garlic and shallots and place the salmon steaks on top. Squeeze over a little lemon juice. Mix the mustard, cream, salt, black pepper and herbs and pour the mixture over the fish.

② Bake in a preheated oven at 180°C/350°F/gas mark 4 for 20 minutes.

③ Serve from the cooking dish with a cucumber salad.

PREPARATION TIME: 10 MINUTES
COOKING TIME: 20 MINUTES
SANCERRE OR MUSCADET TO ACCOMPANY

BAKED BASS WITH WALNUT SAUCE

This recipe can be adapted to any kind of fish (such as sea bass, grouper, grey mullet or bonito). The walnut sauce is extremely nutritious.

—— SERVES 4 ——

	METRIC	IMPERIAL	AMERICAN
Garlic cloves, chopped	2	2	2
Chopped fresh coriander (cilantro)	30 ml	2 tbsp	2 tbsp
Olive oil	90 ml	6 tbsp	6 tbsp
Salt and freshly ground black pepper			
Whole bass, filleted and skinned	1½ kg	3 lb	3 lb
Jerusalem artichokes, sliced	450 g	1 lb	4 cups
For the walnut sauce:			
Walnuts	150 g	5 oz	1¼ cups
Juice of 1 lemon			
Green chilli, seeded and chopped	½	½	½
Olive oil	30 ml	2 tbsp	2 tbsp
Water	60 ml	4 tbsp	4 tbsp
Double (heavy) cream or yoghurt (optional)	30 ml	2 tbsp	2 tbsp

① Pound the garlic and coriander with the olive oil and salt and pepper into a paste. Rub the fish fillets with this mixture.

② Place the fish in an earthenware gratin dish and cover with sliced Jerusalem artichokes. Cover with foil and bake in a preheated oven for 20 minutes at 180°C/350°F/gas mark 4.

③ Meanwhile, prepare the sauce by pounding to a paste or liquidising the walnuts, lemon juice, chilli, olive oil and water. A little cream or yoghurt can also be added if you wish. Serve the fish with the sauce offered separately.

PREPARATION TIME: 25 MINUTES
COOKING TIME: 20 MINUTES
GERMAN MOSELLE TO ACCOMPANY

BAKED SEA BREAM WITH TAHINI

The sea bream in this Arab dish can be replaced by other fish such as trout, haddock, pollack or cod.

—— SERVES 4 ——

	METRIC	IMPERIAL	AMERICAN
Olive oil			
Onions, sliced	450 g	1 lb	1 lb
New potatoes, sliced	450 g	1 lb	1 lb
Sea bream, filleted and scaled, about 150 g/5 oz each	4	4	4
Salt and freshly ground black pepper			
For the tahini:			
Sesame seeds	150 g	5 oz	1¼ cups
Water	300 ml	½ pt	1¼ cups
Juice and grated rind of 2 lemons			
Garlic cloves, chopped	2	2	2
Salt	5 ml	1 tsp	1 tsp
Green chilli, seeded and chopped	1	1	1
White wine vinegar	45 ml	3 tbsp	3 tbsp
Snipped fresh chives	30 ml	2 tbsp	2 tbsp

① Heat the oil in a pan and fry (sauté) the onions for 4 minutes, stirring over a low heat until softened but not browned.

② Place the potatoes in the bottom of a casserole (Dutch oven) and cover with the onions. Place the fish on top and season with salt and pepper.

③ Pound the tahini ingredients together with a pestle and mortar or purée in a blender or food processor. Spread the sauce over the fish.

④ Cover with foil and bake in a preheated oven at 180°C/ 350°F/gas mark 4 for 20 minutes.

PREPARATION TIME: 25 MINUTES
COOKING TIME: 20 MINUTES
RETSINA IS THE IDEAL ACCOMPANIMENT, OR A WHITE RIOJA

POULTRY CASSEROLES

The term 'poultry' is applied to all domesticated birds that have been bred and fattened for the table, including chicken, poussins, ducks, geese, turkeys, guinea fowl, pigeon and quail. All types can be cooked in similar ways. A classic Coq au Vin, for instance, could be produced using pheasant, guinea fowl, turkey or even duck, although the latter would be more fatty.

For the best flavour, choose free-range or corn-fed birds and look for a chicken with tender flesh which is elastic to the touch, not flabby. It should have a well-rounded breast, fleshy thighs, well-distributed fat and a soft and flexible breast bone.

There are two types of chicken casserole dishes: the pot-roasted casserole, which we chefs call *poellé*, using the whole bird cooked in an oval casserole (Dutch oven) just large enough to hold the bird. The second style is usually referred to as oven sautéed, where the raw portions of poultry are cooked in a preheated oven with enough liquid to provide a good sauce. Both types of dish are cooked covered with a lid, which is only removed to brown the bird.

There is also a difference between brown and white sauce casseroles. For the latter, cream is added and the chicken is cooked without colouring the skin, whereas in brown sauces, the skin is coloured before braising. The true flavour of the birds emanates from the fatty skin, so it is essential that you do not remove it before cooking.

BASQUE CHICKEN CASSEROLE

—— SERVES 4–6 ——

	METRIC	IMPERIAL	METRIC
Chicken portions	8	8	8
Seasoned plain (all-purpose) flour	45 ml	3 tbsp	3 tbsp
Olive oil	60 ml	4 tbsp	4 tbsp
Red (bell) pepper, seeded and sliced	I	I	I
Green pepper, seeded and sliced	I	I	I
Yellow pepper, seeded and sliced	I	I	I
Spanish onion, sliced	I	I	I
Garlic clove, chopped	I	I	I
Dry white wine	300 ml	½ pt	I ¼ cups
Mushrooms, sliced	I00 g	4 oz	4 oz
Tomatoes, skinned, seeded and chopped	3	3	3
Chopped fresh parsley	45 ml	3 tbsp	3 tbsp
Salt	5 ml	I tsp	I tsp
Freshly ground black pepper	5 ml	I tsp	I tsp
Dry white wine	I50 ml	¼ pt	⅔ cup
Water	I00 ml	3½ fl oz	scant I cup
Chicken stock cube, crumbled	I	I	I
Boiled rice, to serve			

① Coat the chicken with the flour, shaking off any surplus.

② Heat the oil in a flameproof casserole (Dutch oven) and brown the chicken pieces for 10 minutes. Add the peppers, onion, garlic, wine and mushrooms.

③ Cover and braise in a preheated oven at 200°C/400°F/gas mark 6 for 15 minutes.

④ Stir in all the remaining ingredients, cover and cook for a further 10 minutes or until the chicken is cooked through.

⑤ Serve with boiled rice.

PREPARATION TIME: 15 MINUTES
COOKING TIME: 35 MINUTES
SPANISH WHITE WINE TO ACCOMPANY

CHANNEL ISLANDS CHICKEN

This chicken dish uses Jersey cream and is comparable to, if not better than, the famous Poulet Normande.

—— SERVES 4 ——

	METRIC	IMPERIAL	AMERICAN
Chicken breasts	4	4	4
Seasoned plain (all-purpose) flour	30 ml	2 tbsp	2 tbsp
Butter or margarine	50 g	2 oz	¼ cup
Oil	15 ml	1 tbsp	1 tbsp
Button mushrooms	8	8	8
Button (pearl) onions	8	8	8
Salt	5 ml	1 tsp	1 tsp
White pepper	5 ml	1 tsp	1 tsp
A pinch of dried thyme			
Grated nutmeg	2.5 ml	½ tsp	½ tsp
Medium white vermouth	150 ml	¼ pt	⅔ cup
Double (heavy) cream	150 ml	¼ pt	⅔ cup
Jersey new potatoes, to serve			

① Coat the chicken pieces with seasoned flour and shake off the surplus.

② Heat the butter or margarine and oil in a flameproof casserole (Dutch oven) and fry (sauté) the chicken pieces to develop their flavour without allowing them to brown. Add the mushrooms and onions and cook for 2 minutes. Blend in all the remaining ingredients except the cream.

③ Cover and cook in a preheated oven at 180°C/350°F/gas mark 4 for 1 hour.

④ Just before serving, stir in the cream and adjust the seasoning to taste. Serve with Jersey new potatoes.

PREPARATION TIME: 10 MINUTES
COOKING TIME: 1 HOUR
HOCK OR AN ALSACE WINE TO ACCOMPANY

CHICKEN WITH PORT WINE

If you prefer to use red wine, choose a good Burgundy such as Côtes de Beaune Villages.

—— SERVES 4 ——

	METRIC	IMPERIAL	AMERICAN
Chicken legs, separated into drumsticks and thighs	4	4	4
Seasoned plain (all-purpose) flour	10 ml	2 tsp	2 tsp
Oil	60 ml	4 tbsp	4 tbsp
Back bacon rashers (slices), rinded and diced	2	2	2
Button (pearl) onions	8	8	8
Button mushrooms	8	8	8
Ruby port or full red wine	300 ml	½ pt	1¼ cups
Water	150 ml	¼ pt	⅔ cup
Yeast extract	5 ml	1 tsp	1 tsp
Ground mixed (apple-pie) spice	2.5 ml	½ tsp	½ tsp
Garlic cloves, chopped	2	2	2
Tomato purée (paste)	15 ml	1 tbsp	1 tbsp
Dried thyme	5 ml	1 tsp	1 tsp
Chopped fresh parsley	15 ml	1 tbsp	1 tbsp
Chopped fresh tarragon	15 ml	1 tbsp	1 tbsp
Noodles or pasta shells, to serve			

1. Coat the chicken pieces in the flour, shaking off the surplus.

2. Heat the oil in a flameproof casserole (Dutch oven) and brown the chicken pieces and bacon together for 3 minutes. Add the onions and continue to cook until slightly golden. Add the mushrooms. Blend in all the remaining ingredients except the fresh herbs.

3. Cover and braise gently for 1 hour at 180°C/350°F/gas mark 4. Sprinkle with the herbs just before serving.

4. Serve with noodles or pasta shells.

PREPARATION TIME: 20 MINUTES
COOKING TIME: 1 HOUR
CHABLIS OR ROSÉ WINE TO ACCOMPANY

PORTUGUESE CHICKEN CASSEROLE
—— SERVES 4 ——

	METRIC	IMPERIAL	AMERICAN
Seasoned plain (all-purpose) flour	30 ml	2 tbsp	2 tbsp
Paprika	5 ml	I tsp	I tsp
Breasts of chicken, halved	4	4	4
Olive oil	60 ml	4 tbsp	4 tbsp
Spanish onion, chopped	I	I	I
Tomatoes, skinned, seeded and chopped	4	4	4
Tomato purée (paste)	15 ml	I tbsp	I tbsp
Spanish white wine	150 ml	¼ pt	⅔ cup
Water	100 ml	3½ fl oz	scant ½ cup
Stuffed Spanish olives	8	8	8
Salt	5 ml	I tsp	I tsp
Freshly ground black pepper	5 ml	I tsp	I tsp
Chicken stock cube, crumbled	I	I	I
Garlic clove, crushed	I	I	I
A pinch of saffron powder			
Chopped fresh coriander (cilantro)	30 ml	2 tbsp	2 tbsp
Boiled rice, to serve			

① Combine the seasoned flour and paprika and use to coat the chicken pieces, shaking off any surplus.

② Heat the oil in a flameproof casserole (Dutch oven) and brown the chicken pieces for 8 minutes. Add the onion and cook for a further 2 minutes, stirring well. Stir in all the remaining ingredients except the coriander.

③ Cover and braise in a preheated oven at 180°C/350°F/gas mark 4 for 1½ hours.

④ Sprinkle on the chopped coriander and serve with rice.

PREPARATION TIME: 15 MINUTES
COOKING TIME: 1½ HOURS
CHABLIS OR SPANISH ROSÉ TO ACCOMPANY

BARCELONA CHICKEN

—— SERVES 4 ——

	METRIC	IMPERIAL	AMERICAN
Oil	90 ml	6 tbsp	6 tbsp
Streaky bacon rashers (slices), rinded and diced	2	2	2
Chicken breasts, skinned and cut into 2.5 cm/1 in pieces	450 g	1 lb	1 lb
Red onion, chopped	1	1	1
Green chilli, seeded and chopped	1	1	1
Garlic cloves, chopped	4	4	4
Seasoned plain (all-purpose) flour	45 ml	3 tbsp	3 tbsp
Spanish white wine	300 ml	½ pt	1¼ cups
Tomatoes, skinned, seeded and chopped	6	6	6
Celery stick, chopped	1	1	1
A pinch of saffron powder			
Salt and freshly ground black pepper			
Fresh basil leaves, chopped	6	6	6
Boiled rice or noodles, to serve			

① Heat the oil in a flameproof casserole (Dutch oven) and brown the bacon and chicken for 15 minutes. Add the onion, chilli and garlic and stir for 30 seconds.

② Sprinkle in the seasoned flour to absorb the surplus oil. Blend in the white wine and boil for 4 minutes. Stir in the tomatoes. Add the celery, saffron, salt and pepper.

③ Cover and braise in a preheated oven at 180°C/350°F/gas mark 4 for 35–40 minutes.

④ Sprinkle with the chopped basil leaves and serve with boiled rice or noodles.

PREPARATION TIME: 30 MINUTES
COOKING TIME: 35–40 MINUTES
SPANISH WHITE WINE TO ACCOMPANY

COCONUT CHICKEN CURRY WITH PINEAPPLE

—— SERVES 4 ——

	METRIC	IMPERIAL	AMERICAN
Desiccated (shredded) coconut, lightly toasted	30 ml	2 tbsp	2 tbsp
Curry powder	30 ml	2 tbsp	2 tbsp
Ground cinnamon	1.5 ml	¼ tsp	¼ tsp
Ground ginger	5 ml	1 tsp	1 tsp
Chicken legs, boned and diced	4	4	4
Chicken breasts, boned and diced	2	2	2
Oil	75 ml	5 tbsp	5 tbsp
Onion, chopped	1	1	1
Garlic clove, chopped	1	1	1
Water	450 ml	¾ pt	2 cups
Juice and grated rind of 1 lemon			
Clear honey	30 ml	2 tbsp	2 tbsp
Tomato purée (paste)	7.5 ml	½ tbsp	½ tbsp
Salt and freshly ground black pepper	2.5 ml	½ tsp	½ tsp
Pineapple, fresh or canned, cubed	100 g	4 oz	4 oz
Boiled rice and poppadoms, to serve			

① Mix the coconut, curry powder, cinnamon and ginger and rub over the chicken pieces. Shake off any surplus.

② Heat the oil in a flameproof casserole (Dutch oven) and fry (sauté) the chicken for about 5 minutes, turning frequently, until golden all over. Add the onion and garlic and cook for 1 minute. Pour in the water, lemon juice and rind, honey and tomato purée. Season with salt and pepper.

③ Cover and cook in a preheated oven at 180°C/350°F/gas mark 4 for 45 minutes.

④ Stir in the pineapple cubes and heat for 5–10 minutes.

⑤ Serve with boiled rice and poppadoms.

PREPARATION TIME: 15 MINUTES

COOKING TIME: 45 MINUTES

CHILLED FRUIT JUICE OR INDIAN LAGER TO ACCOMPANY

FARMHOUSE CHICKEN CASSEROLE

This casserole is equally good made with small turkey breasts. The potatoes should be about the size of eggs.

—— SERVES 4 ——

	METRIC	IMPERIAL	AMERICAN
Butter or margarine	25 g	1 oz	2 tbsp
Oil	30 ml	2 tbsp	2 tbsp
Lean bacon rashers (slices), rinded and diced	100 g	4 oz	4 oz
Carrots, peeled and diced	2	2	2
Onion, chopped	1	1	1
Leeks, white part only, sliced	2	2	2
Celery stick, sliced	1	1	1
Chicken breasts, skinned	4	4	4
Water	400 ml	14 fl oz	1¾ cups
Chicken stock cubes, crumbled	2	2	2
A sprig of thyme			
Mushrooms, quartered	225 g	8 oz	8 oz
Juice and grated rind of 1 lemon			
Small potatoes	8	8	8
Salt and freshly ground black pepper			
Egg yolk	1	1	1
Double (heavy) cream	120 ml	4 fl oz	½ cup
Cornflour (cornstarch)	5 ml	1 tsp	1 tsp
Grated nutmeg	2.5 ml	½ tsp	½ tsp

① Heat the butter or margarine and oil in a flameproof casserole (Dutch oven) and stir-fry the bacon, carrots, onion, leeks and celery for 5 minutes. Add the chicken and toss for 3 minutes.

② Add the water, stock cubes, thyme, mushrooms, lemon juice and rind and potatoes. Season and cook gently for 25 minutes until the meat is tender.

③ Blend together the egg yolk, cream, cornflour and nutmeg and add 120 ml/4 fl oz/½ cup of the cooking juices. Blend this mixture into the rest of the gravy and heat through until thickened but do not boil.

④ Season to taste with salt and pepper before serving.

PREPARATION TIME: 25 MINUTES
COOKING TIME: 30 MINUTES
ROSÉ, MUSCADET OR CHABLIS TO ACCOMPANY

CHICKEN BEAUJOLAIS
—— SERVES 4 ——

	METRIC	IMPERIAL	AMERICAN
Chicken, cut into 8 portions	1.5 kg	3 lb	3 lb
Seasoned plain (all-purpose) flour	45 ml	3 tbsp	3 tbsp
Oil	45 ml	3 tbsp	3 tbsp
Butter or margarine	50 g	2 oz	¼ cup
Onion, chopped	1	1	1
Carrot, diced	1	1	1
Beaujolais Nouveau or light red wine	600 ml	1 pt	2½ cups
Chicken stock cube, crumbled	1	1	1
A sprig of thyme			
Garlic cloves, chopped	2	2	2
Tomato purée (paste)	15 ml	1 tbsp	1 tbsp
Button (pearl) onions	12	12	12
Button mushrooms	12	12	12
Sugar	5 ml	1 tsp	1 tsp
Salt and freshly ground black pepper			
Ground mace	2.5 ml	½ tsp	½ tsp
Mixed (apple-pie) spice	1.5 ml	¼ tsp	¼ tsp
Cornflour (cornstarch)	5 ml	1 tsp	1 tsp
Water	45 ml	3 tbsp	3 tbsp
Yeast extract	5 ml	1 tsp	1 tsp
Chopped fresh parsley	30 ml	2 tbsp	2 tbsp
Fresh vegetables, to serve			

① Rub the chicken pieces in seasoned flour and shake off the surplus.

② Heat the oil and half the butter or margarine in a flameproof casserole (Dutch oven) and brown the chicken for 15 minutes. Add the onion and carrot and toss for 2 minutes. Pour in the wine, bring to the boil and simmer for 5 minutes.

③ Add the stock cube, thyme, garlic and tomato purée and simmer for 4 minutes. Season with salt and pepper.

④ Cover and cook in a preheated oven at 180°C/350°F/gas mark 4 for 45 minutes until tender.

⑤ Meanwhile, boil the onions for 4 minutes and the mushrooms for 30 seconds, then drain.

⑦ Heat the remaining butter or margarine with the sugar until it becomes sticky. Toss the onions and mushrooms in this butterscotch mixture to glaze for 2 minutes. Season with salt, pepper, mace and mixed spice.

⑦ When the chicken is cooked, stir together the cornflour, water and yeast extract and add to the casserole. Simmer on top of the stove for 4 minutes until thickened.

⑧ Sprinkle with parsley and serve with the glazed onions and mushrooms and fresh vegetables.

PREPARATION TIME: 30 MINUTES
COOKING TIME: 45 MINUTES
BEAUJOLAIS TO ACCOMPANY

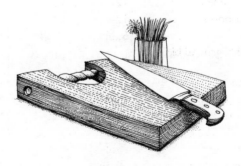

COCK-A-LEEKIE CASSEROLE

—— SERVES 4 ——

	METRIC	IMPERIAL	AMERICAN
Chicken breasts	4	4	4
Seasoned plain (all-purpose) flour	30 ml	2 tbsp	2 tbsp
Butter or margarine	50 g	2 oz	¼ cup
Back bacon rashers (slices), rinded	4	4	4
Small leeks, white parts only	8	8	8
Salt	5 ml	I tsp	I tsp
Freshly ground black pepper	5 ml	I tsp	I tsp
Medium sherry	300 ml	½ pt	I ¼ cups
Chicken stock cube	I	I	I
Water	I50 ml	¼ pt	⅔ cup

① Coat the chicken breasts with seasoned flour and shake off the surplus.

② Heat the butter or margarine in a flameproof casserole (Dutch oven) and fry (sauté) the chicken quickly to develop its flavour without allowing it to brown. Remove from the casserole.

③ Place the chicken, bacon and leeks in layers in the casserole. Season with salt and pepper and add the sherry and stock.

④ Cover and braise in a preheated oven at 180°C/350°F/gas mark 4 for 1½ hours until tender.

PREPARATION TIME: 15 MINUTES

COOKING TIME: 1½ HOURS

MUSCADET OR CHABLIS TO ACCOMPANY

TURKEY CASSEROLE WITH TARRAGON

This simple dish of turkey cooked in its own stock without colouring is a great favourite with many people.

—— SERVES 4 ——

	METRIC	IMPERIAL	AMERICAN
Turkey breast, cut into large chunks	750 g	1½ lb	1½ lb
Water	300 ml	½ pt	1¼ cups
Dry white wine	300 ml	½ pt	1¼ cups
Chicken stock cube	1	1	1
Coarsely chopped fresh tarragon	30 ml	2 tbsp	2 tbsp
Baby carrots	150 g	5 oz	5 oz
Celery sticks, cut into fingers	2	2	2
Small leeks, white part only	4	4	4
Mangetout (snow peas)	8	8	8
Spring onions (scallions)	4	4	4
A sprig of thyme			
Salt	5 ml	1 tsp	1 tsp
Black peppercorns, crushed	6	6	6
New potatoes, to serve			

① Put all the ingredients in a casserole (Dutch oven) and season with the salt and crushed peppercorns. Cover and cook in a preheated oven at 200°C/400°F/gas mark 6 for 1 hour.

② Serve with new potatoes.

PREPARATION TIME: 20 MINUTES
COOKING TIME: 1 HOUR
HOCK OR MOSELLE TO ACCOMPANY

CASSEROLED TURKEY PATTIES WITH CRANBERRY SAUCE

—— SERVES 4 ——

	METRIC	IMPERIAL	AMERICAN
For the turkey patties:			
Minced (ground) turkey	225 g	8 oz	8 oz
Pork sausagemeat	150 g	5 oz	5 oz
Egg, beaten	1	1	1
Canned, frozen or cooked chestnuts	100 g	4 oz	4 oz
Chopped fresh parsley	15 ml	1 tbsp	1 tbsp
Onion, chopped	1	1	1
Whisky	5 ml	1 tsp	1 tsp
Salt and freshly ground black pepper			
Seasoned plain (all-purpose) flour	15 ml	1 tbsp	1 tbsp
Butter or margarine	50 g	2 oz	¼ cup
Oil	30 ml	2 tbsp	2 tbsp
For the cranberry sauce:			
Ginger wine	150 ml	¼ pt	⅔ cup
Sugar	50 g	2 oz	¼ cup
Cornflour (cornstarch)	5 ml	1 tsp	1 tsp
Water	30 ml	2 tbsp	2 tbsp
Cranberries	225 g	8 oz	8 oz
Salt and freshly ground black pepper			
Brussels sprouts, to serve			

① Combine all the patty ingredients except the seasoned flour, butter or margarine and oil. Divide into four large balls, then flatten and shape like fish cakes. Coat with seasoned flour.

② Heat the butter or margarine and oil in a shallow flameproof casserole (Dutch oven) and brown the patties for 4 minutes on each side. Pour off the fat.

③ Liquidise all the ingredients for the cranberry sauce except the cranberries and pour into the dish.

④ Cover and bake in a preheated oven at 200°C/400°F/ gas mark 6 for 15–20 minutes until the sauce is thick.

⑤ Stir in the cranberries, season to taste with salt and pepper and cook for a further 5 minutes until heated through.

⑥ Serve with Brussels sprouts.

PREPARATION TIME: 20 MINUTES
COOKING TIME: 15–20 MINUTES
ROSÉ OR MUSCADET TO ACCOMPANY

DUCK WITH CHICK PEAS

This casserole of duck with chick peas (garbanzos) has been popular in Algeria for many years. It is extremely nourishing and tasty.

—— SERVES 4 ——

	METRIC	IMPERIAL	AMERICAN
Whole duck, cut into 8 portions	1.75 kg	4 lb	4 lb
Seasoned plain (all-purpose) flour	30 ml	2 tbsp	2 tbsp
Oil	60 ml	4 tbsp	4 tbsp
Orange juice	300 ml	½ pt	1¼ cups
Grenadine	150 ml	¼ pt	⅔ cup
Yeast extract	15 ml	1 tbsp	1 tbsp
Duck stock or water	300 ml	½ pt	1¼ cups
Salt	5 ml	1 tsp	1 tsp
A pinch of chilli powder			
A pinch of ground cumin			
Garlic cloves, chopped	2	2	2
Onion, chopped	1	1	1
Canned or cooked chick peas	225 g	8 oz	8 oz
Fennel bulb, thinly sliced	1	1	1
Couscous or rice, to serve			

① Coat the duck pieces in seasoned flour and shake off the surplus.

② Heat the oil in a flameproof casserole (Dutch oven) and brown the duck pieces all over for 5 minutes. Stir in all the remaining ingredients except the chick peas and the fennel.

③ Cover and braise in a preheated oven at 190°C/375°F/gas mark 5 for 45 minutes.

④ Remove the surplus fat, then stir in the chick peas and fennel, reduce the oven temperature to 160°C/325°F/gas mark 3 and cook for a further 45 minutes.

⑤ Skim off the fat and serve with couscous or rice.

PREPARATION TIME: 10 MINUTES
COOKING TIME: 1½ HOURS
RICH, RED ALGERIAN WINE TO ACCOMPANY

PIGEON IN BROWN ALE

Pigeon is a delicacy, especially if domesticated and well-fed. Young birds are tender and, like grouse, should not be overcooked, but older birds need long simmering in a casserole.

——— SERVES 4 ———

	METRIC	IMPERIAL	AMERICAN
Pigeons, cut into halves	4	4	4
Seasoned plain (all-purpose) flour	30 ml	2 tbsp	2 tbsp
Oil	45 ml	3 tbsp	3 tbsp
Salt	5 ml	I tsp	I tsp
Freshly ground black pepper	2.5 ml	½ tsp	½ tsp
Brown ale	600 ml	I pt	2½ cups
Yeast extract	15 ml	I tbsp	I tbsp
Juice of I lemon			
Light brown sugar	15 ml	I tbsp	I tbsp
Tomato purée (paste)	5 ml	I tsp	I tsp
Cooked fresh or frozen peas	225 g	8 oz	8 oz
Cooked spring onions (scallions)	8	8	8
Mashed potato, to serve			

① Coat the pigeons with seasoned flour and shake off any surplus.

② Heat the oil in a flameproof casserole (Dutch oven) and brown the pigeons all over for 10 minutes. Stir in all the remaining ingredients.

③ Cover and braise in a preheated oven at 160°C/325°F/gas mark 3 for 1½ hours until the meat falls off the bones.

④ Adjust the seasoning, arrange the cooked peas and spring onions over the pigeons and serve with mashed potato.

PREPARATION TIME: 15 MINUTES
COOKING TIME: 1½ HOURS
LIGHT ROSÉ WINE OR CIDER TO ACCOMPANY

LAMB CASSEROLES

Spring lamb has become traditional at Easter and Passover celebrations. It is also a most versatile meat, happily combining with a whole variety of other flavours, from herbs and spices to fruit and vegetables.

The most tender cuts of lamb are best end (cutlets), loin and leg, then shoulder, middle neck, scrag and breast. For hot-pot cookery, cuts from the middle neck and shoulders are usually the best pieces, provided the fat is removed before cooking.

LAMB AND AUBERGINE CASSEROLE

This lamb dish, redolent of ratatouille, has always been very popular in Mediterranean cuisine. You can use middle neck instead of chump chops, if you prefer.

—— SERVES 4 ——

	METRIC	IMPERIAL	AMERICAN
Oil	30 ml	2 tbsp	2 tbsp
Lamb chump chops	4	4	4
Aubergine (eggplant), peeled and sliced	I	I	I
Green (bell) pepper, split, seeded and cut into small squares	I	I	I
Tomato, skinned, seeded and chopped	I	I	I
Onion, sliced	I	I	I
Garlic cloves, crushed	2	2	2
A pinch of saffron powder			
Salt and freshly ground black pepper			
Water or rosé wine	300 ml	½ pt	I¼ cups
Rice or pasta, to serve			

① Heat the oil in a flameproof casserole (Dutch oven) and brown the chops for 5 minutes. Add the aubergine, pepper, tomato, onion, garlic, saffron and seasoning, and cover with water or wine.

② Braise in a preheated oven at 180°C/350°F/gas mark 4 for 1¼ hours.

③ Serve with rice or pasta.

PREPARATION TIME: 15 MINUTES
COOKING TIME: 1¼ HOURS
PROVENÇAL ROSÉ TO ACCOMPANY

LANCASHIRE HOT-POT

This is a traditional lamb dish from the north of England. Only potatoes and other white vegetables should be used with the chump chops or pieces of neck.

—— SERVES 4–6 ——

	METRIC	IMPERIAL	AMERICAN
Oil	30 ml	2 tbsp	2 tbsp
Neck of lamb or chump chops	I kg	2¼ lb	2¼ lb
Onion, sliced	I	I	I
Parsnips, sliced	2	2	2
Celery stick, sliced	I	I	I
Potatoes, sliced	450 g	I lb	I lb
Water	I litre	1¾ pts	4¼ cups
Bouquet garni	I	I	I
Salt	5 ml	I tsp	I tsp
Coarsely ground black pepper	1.5 ml	¼ tsp	¼ tsp

① Pour the oil into the bottom of the casserole (Dutch oven) and layer the meat and vegetables alternately until three-quarters full. Top up with water and add the bouquet garni. Season with salt and pepper.

② Cover with a lid and braise in a preheated oven at 180°C/ 350°F/gas mark 4 for 1¼ hours.

PREPARATION TIME: 15 MINUTES

COOKING TIME: 1¼ HOURS

FRUITY ENGLISH WHITE WINE TO ACCOMPANY

BRAISED LAMB LOAF WITH HARICOT BEANS

This is a delicious and economical Latin American dish.

—— SERVES 4 ——

	METRIC	IMPERIAL	AMERICAN
Corn oil	60 ml	4 tbsp	4 tbsp
Minced (ground) lamb	225 g	8 oz	8 oz
Egg, beaten	1	1	1
Cooked or canned sweetcorn (corn) kernels	150 g	5 oz	1¼ cups
Cooked haricot (navy) beans	100 g	4 oz	1 cup
Tomato purée (paste)	15 ml	1 tbsp	1 tbsp
Chilli, seeded and chopped	1	1	1
Salt	5 ml	1 tsp	1 tsp
Fresh mint leaves, chopped	3	3	3
Desiccated (shredded) coconut	5 ml	1 tsp	1 tsp
Tomato salad, to serve			

① Pour the oil in a small casserole (Dutch oven). Combine all the ingredients and place in the casserole, pressing down well.

② Cover and braise in a preheated oven at 180°C/350°F/gas mark 4 for 1 hour.

③ When cooked, leave to cool until completely cold, then slice and serve with a tomato salad.

PREPARATION TIME: 5 MINUTES PLUS COOLING

COOKING TIME: 1 HOUR

HEARTY, RED CHILEAN WINE TO ACCOMPANY

LAMB AND POTATO CASSEROLE

Boned neck or breast of lamb is very cheap but this dish is as tasty as it is economical.

—— SERVES 4 ——

	METRIC	IMPERIAL	AMERICAN
Olive oil	45 ml	3 tbsp	3 tbsp
Breast or neck of lamb, boned	I kg	2¼ lb	2¼ lb
Streaky bacon rashers (slices), rinded and diced	4	4	4
Button (pearl) onions	8	8	8
Button mushrooms	8	8	8
Potatoes, cubed	450 g	I lb	I lb
Medium sherry	150 ml	¼ pt	⅔ cup
Worcestershire sauce	5 ml	I tsp	I tsp
Water	300 ml	½ pt	1¼ cups
Lamb or chicken stock cube, crumbled	I	I	I
Salt and freshly ground black pepper			
Tomato purée (paste)	5 ml	I tsp	I tsp
Cauliflower cheese and green vegetables, to serve			

① Heat the oil in a flameproof casserole (Dutch oven) and brown the lamb for 6 minutes. Add the bacon, onions, mushrooms, potatoes, sherry, Worcestershire sauce, water and stock cube. Season to taste with salt and pepper. Bring to the boil and add the tomato purée.

② Cover and braise in a preheated oven at 180°C/350°F/gas mark 4 for 1½ hours.

③ Serve with cauliflower cheese and green vegetables.

PREPARATION TIME: 15 MINUTES
COOKING TIME: 1½ HOURS
BEAUJOLAIS NOUVEAU OR BULGARIAN CABERNET RED WINE
TO ACCOMPANY

HUNTER'S LAMB CASSEROLE
—— SERVES 6 ——

	METRIC	IMPERIAL	AMERICAN
Oil	60 ml	4 tbsp	4 tbsp
Onions, diced	150 g	5 oz	5 oz
Red (bell) pepper, seeded and cubed	1	1	1
Green pepper, seeded and cubed	1	1	1
Garlic cloves, chopped	2	2	2
Shoulder of lamb, skinned and cubed	1 kg	2¼ lb	2¼ lb
Chopped fresh tarragon	30 ml	2 tbsp	2 tbsp
Crushed fresh rosemary leaves	5 ml	1 tsp	1 tsp
Button mushrooms, diced or quartered	150 g	5 oz	5 oz
Plain (all-purpose) flour	15 g	½ oz	2 tbsp
Water	150 ml	¼ pt	⅔ cup
Dry vermouth	120 ml	4 fl oz	½ cup
Salt and freshly ground black pepper			
Cooked or canned broad (lima) beans	150 g	5 oz	1¼ cups
Boiled rice or polenta, to serve			

① Heat the oil in a flameproof casserole (Dutch oven) and fry (sauté) the onion until softened but not browned. Add the peppers and garlic and fry, stirring, for 1 minute.

② Add the meat, herbs and mushrooms. Cook for a further 5 minutes, stirring continuously, until all the liquid has evaporated. Sprinkle with the flour, stir, and add the water, vermouth and salt and pepper.

③ Cover and braise in a preheated oven at 180°C/350°F/gas mark 4 for 1 hour.

④ Mix in the broad beans and heat through for a further 5 minutes.

⑤ Serve with rice or polenta.

PREPARATION TIME: 25 MINUTES
COOKING TIME: 1 HOUR
BEAUJOLAIS OR HEARTY SPANISH RED WINE TO ACCOMPANY

SPANISH-STYLE LAMB

—— SERVES 6 ——

	METRIC	IMPERIAL	AMERICAN
Olive oil	45 ml	3 tbsp	3 tbsp
Lean shoulder of lamb, boned and diced	I kg	2¼ lb	2¼ lb
Onions, diced	450 g	I lb	I lb
Garlic cloves, chopped	2	2	2
A pinch of saffron powder			
Plain (all-purpose) flour	15 ml	I tbsp	I tbsp
Tomatoes, skinned, seeded and chopped	450 g	I lb	I lb
Paprika	5 ml	I tsp	I tsp
Ground cumin	5 ml	I tsp	I tsp
Ground cloves	2.5 ml	½ tsp	½ tsp
Freshly ground black pepper	5 ml	I tsp	I tsp
Water	500 ml	17 fl oz	2¼ cups
Red wine	500 ml	17 fl oz	2¼ cups
Cooked butterfly pasta	100 g	4 oz	I cup
Chopped fresh parsley	45 ml	3 tbsp	3 tbsp

① Heat the oil in a flameproof casserole (Dutch oven) and brown the meat for 5 minutes. Add the onion, garlic and saffron and toss for 1 minute. Stir in the flour. Blend in the tomatoes, paprika and all the spices. Finally, stir in the water and wine.

② Cover and braise in a preheated oven at 180°C/350°F/gas mark 4 for 1 hour until the meat is tender.

③ Check and adjust the seasoning, stir in the pasta, heat through and serve sprinkled with parsley.

PREPARATION TIME: 20 MINUTES

COOKING TIME: 1 HOUR

ROSÉ OR FRUITY SPANISH RED WINE TO ACCOMPANY

ALGERIAN LAMB AND PUMPKIN CASSEROLE

This is a little-known but delicious African stew. I would suggest that you use about 450 g/1 lb of pumpkin cubes but you can vary this to suit your own taste.

—— SERVES 6 ——

	METRIC	IMPERIAL	AMERICAN
Shoulder of lamb, trimmed and cubed	1 kg	2¼ lb	2¼ lb
Seasoned plain (all-purpose) flour	30 ml	2 tbsp	2 tbsp
Oil	60 ml	4 tbsp	4 tbsp
Onions, chopped	2	2	2
Garlic cloves, chopped	3	3	3
Green chilli, seeded and chopped	1	1	1
Piece of fresh root ginger, peeled and chopped	2.5 cm	1 in	1 in
Tomatoes, skinned, seeded and chopped	4	4	4
Water	600 ml	1 pt	2½ cups
Pumpkin, skinned and cut into 2.5 cm/1 in cubes	1	1	1
Salt and freshly ground black pepper			
Potatoes or rice, to serve			

① Dust the lamb in the seasoned flour and shake off any surplus. Heat the oil in a flameproof casserole (Dutch oven) and fry (sauté) the onions, garlic and chilli for 2 minutes. Add the ginger and lamb and let it brown for 2 more minutes while tossing and stirring. Add the tomatoes, water and pumpkin.

② Cover and braise in a preheated oven at 180°C/350°F/gas mark 4 for 1½ hours.

③ Season when the casserole is cooked and serve with potatoes or rice.

PREPARATION TIME: 20 MINUTES

COOKING TIME: 1½ HOURS

HEARTY ALGERIAN OR SPANISH RED WINE TO ACCOMPANY

LAMB CUTLET AND POTATO HOT-POT

This quick and simple meal is best served with a fresh green vegetable.

—— SERVES 4 ——

	METRIC	IMPERIAL	AMERICAN
Oil	60 ml	4 tbsp	4 tbsp
Lamb cutlets, trimmed and chined (boned)	8	8	8
Onion, sliced	1	1	1
Potatoes, sliced	450 g	1 lb	1 lb
Water	300 ml	½ pt	1¼ cups
Stock cube	1	1	1
Salt and freshly ground black pepper			
Cheddar cheese, grated	100 g	4 oz	1 cup

① Heat the oil in a flameproof casserole (Dutch oven) and brown the cutlets for just 1 minute on each side.

② Add the onion and cover with a layer of overlapping sliced potatoes.

③ Bring the water to the boil and stir in the stock cube until dissolved. Pour over the potatoes. Season to taste with salt and pepper. Sprinkle over the grated cheese and bake in a preheated oven at 200°C/400°F/gas mark 6 for 35 minutes.

PREPARATION TIME: 15 MINUTES
COOKING TIME: 35 MINUTES
CIDER OR LAGER TO ACCOMPANY

GREEK-STYLE FRICASSEE OF LAMB WITH LEMON

—— SERVES 4–6 ——

	METRIC	IMPERIAL	AMERICAN
Olive oil	60 ml	4 tbsp	4 tbsp
Leek, white parts only, sliced	I	I	I
Shoulder of lamb, cubed	I kg	2¼ lb	2¼ lb
Plain (all-purpose) flour	15 ml	I tbsp	I tbsp
Salt and freshly ground black pepper			
Water	I litre	1¾ pts	4¼ cups
Fennel bulb, sliced	I	I	I
Cornflour (cornstarch)	15 ml	I tbsp	I tbsp
Egg yolks	3	3	3
Juice and grated rind of I lemon			
Water	90 ml	6 tbsp	6 tbsp
Chopped lemon grass or fresh parsley	30 ml	2 tbsp	2 tbsp
New potatoes or rice, to serve			

① Heat the oil in a flameproof casserole (Dutch oven) and fry (sauté) the leek, stirring, for 1 minute. Add the lamb and fry for 4 minutes without browning. Stir in the flour and season with salt and pepper. Add the water and fennel and bring to the boil. Simmer gently for 1½ hours.

② Whisk together the cornflour, egg yolks, lemon juice and rind and water and gradually add a ladleful of the meat stock. Stir the egg mixture into the stew. Taste and adjust the seasoning.

③ Sprinkle with lemon grass or parsley and serve with new potatoes or rice.

PREPARATION TIME: 25 MINUTES
COOKING TIME: 1½ HOURS
DOMESTICA OR OTHER GREEK WINE TO ACCOMPANY

BRAISED LAMB CHOPS WITH AUBERGINE SAUCE
—— SERVES 4 ——

	METRIC	IMPERIAL	AMERICAN
Salt	5 ml	I tsp	I tsp
Aubergine (eggplant), diced	I	I	I
Oil	60 ml	4 tbsp	4 tbsp
Small lamb chops, trimmed of all fat	8	8	8
Shallots, chopped	2	2	2
Garlic cloves, chopped	2	2	2
Tomatoes, skinned, seeded and chopped	3	3	3
Red wine	150 ml	¼ pt	¾ cup
Salt and freshly ground black pepper			
Cornflour (cornstarch)	5 ml	I tsp	I tsp
Water	45 ml	3 tbsp	3 tbsp
Mozzarella cheese, diced	350 g	12 oz	I½ cups
Snipped fresh chives	45 ml	3 tbsp	3 tbsp

① Sprinkle the salt over the aubergine and leave for 30 minutes to help extract the bitter juice, then rinse in cold water and pat dry with kitchen paper (paper towels).

② Heat 30 ml/2 tbsp of the oil in a flameproof casserole (Dutch oven) and cook the chops for 4 minutes on each side until browned. Remove the chops and keep warm.

③ Heat the remaining oil in the same pan and fry (sauté) the aubergine, shallot and garlic for 5 minutes, stirring and tossing evenly. Add the tomatoes and red wine and season with salt and pepper. Cook, stirring, for 10 minutes.

④ Blend together the cornflour and water to make a paste, then stir into the pan and simmer until thick.

⑤ Return the chops to the pan. Sprinkle the cheese over the top and bake in a preheated oven at 160°C/325°F/gas mark 3 for 30 minutes. Sprinkle over the chives just before serving.

PREPARATION TIME: 25 MINUTES PLUS SALTING OF AUBERGINE
COOKING TIME: 30 MINUTES
MACON OR BEAUJOLAIS TO ACCOMPANY

SPANISH-STYLE LAMB CHOPS

—— SERVES 6 ——

	METRIC	IMPERIAL	AMERICAN
Olive oil	60 ml	4 tbsp	4 tbsp
Potatoes, sliced	450 g	I lb	I lb
Onions, sliced	450 g	I lb	I lb
Tomatoes, skinned, seeded and chopped	450 g	I lb	I lb
Lamb shoulder chops	6	6	6
Green (bell) peppers, seeded and chopped	2	2	2
Garlic bulb, cloves separated and roasted	I	I	I
A pinch of saffron powder			
A pinch of ground cinnamon			
A pinch of ground cloves			
A pinch of ground mace			
Spanish white wine or pale sherry	600 ml	I pt	2½ cups
Salt and freshly ground black pepper			
Mixed green salad, to serve			

① Put the oil in a casserole (Dutch oven) and add alternate layers of potatoes, onions and tomatoes. Place the meat on top. Add the green peppers, roasted garlic, spices and wine or sherry. Season to taste with salt and pepper.

② Cover and bake in a preheated oven at 200°C/400°F/gas mark 6 for 20 minutes, then reduce the oven temperature to 180°C/350°F/gas mark 4 and cook for a further 2 hours.

③ Serve with a mixed green salad.

PREPARATION TIME: 20 MINUTES
COOKING TIME: 2 HOURS 20 MINUTES
MUSCADET OR ROSÉ WINE TO ACCOMPANY

IRISH STEW

The presentation is improved by reserving a few whole potatoes to cook and serve separately as the ones in the stew tend to disintegrate in the gravy.

—— SERVES 6 ——

	METRIC	IMPERIAL	AMERICAN
Onions, sliced	2	2	2
Potatoes, sliced	750 g	1½ lb	1½ lb
Shoulder of lamb, skinned, trimmed and cubed	1 kg	2¼ lb	2¼ lb
Stock cube	1	1	1
Boiling water	600 ml	1 pt	2½ cups
Salt	5 ml	1 tsp	1 tsp
White pepper	1.5 ml	¼ tsp	¼ tsp
A sprig of thyme			
Chopped fresh parsley	30 ml	2 tbsp	2 tbsp

① Place the onions, potatoes and lamb in layers in a casserole (Dutch oven), finishing with a layer of potatoes. Dissolve the stock cube in the water and pour over the dish, then season with salt and pepper and add the sprig of thyme.

② Cover and braise gently in a preheated oven at 180°C/ 350°F/gas mark 4 for 2 hours.

③ Serve in soup plates sprinkled with the parsley.

PREPARATION TIME: 15 MINUTES
COOKING TIME: 2 HOURS
STOUT OR LAGER TO ACCOMPANY

LAMB WITH HARICOT BEANS

This dish was traditionally made with mutton, but lamb works equally well.

—— SERVES 8 ——

	METRIC	IMPERIAL	AMERICAN
Oil	45 ml	3 tbsp	3 tbsp
Shoulder of lamb, cubed	1 kg	2¼ lb	2¼ lb
Streaky bacon, rinded and diced	100 g	4 oz	4 oz
Plain (all-purpose) flour	30 ml	2 tbsp	2 tbsp
Onion, chopped	1	1	1
Garlic cloves, chopped	2	2	2
Carrots, diced	150 g	5 oz	5 oz
Celery sticks, sliced	150 g	5 oz	5 oz
Tomato purée (paste)	60 ml	4 tbsp	4 tbsp
Sugar	5 ml	1 tsp	1 tsp
Salt	5 ml	1 tsp	1 tsp
Freshly ground black pepper	1.5 ml	¼ tsp	¼ tsp
Water	1 litre	1¾ pts	4¼ cups
Can of haricot (navy) beans	400 g	14 oz	1 large

① Heat the oil in a flameproof casserole (Dutch oven) and brown the lamb and bacon for 5 minutes. Sprinkle over the flour, stir, and add all the remaining ingredients except the haricot beans. Bring to the boil.

② Cover and braise in a preheated oven at 180°C/350°F/gas mark 4 for 45 minutes.

③ Add the beans and cook for a further 45 minutes or until the meat and beans are tender. Taste and adjust the seasoning if necessary before serving

PREPARATION TIME: 25 MINUTES

COOKING TIME: 1½ HOURS

STOUT OR CIDER TO ACCOMPANY

ITALIAN LAMB

—— SERVES 4-6 ——

	METRIC	IMPERIAL	AMERICAN
Leg of lamb, boned	1 kg	2¼ lb	2¼ lb
Back bacon, rinded	225 g	8 oz	8 oz
Green chilli, seeded	1	1	1
Red chilli, seeded	1	1	1
Fettucine pasta	225 g	8 oz	8 oz
Olive or corn oil	60 ml	4 tbsp	4 tbsp
Garlic cloves, chopped	2	2	2
Onions, thinly sliced	150 g	5 oz	5 oz
Water	150 ml	¼ pt	⅔ cup
Dry white wine	150 ml	¼ pt	⅔ cup
Double (heavy) cream	300 ml	½ pt	1¼ cups
Salt and freshly ground black pepper			
Parmesan or any hard cheese, grated	150 g	5 oz	1¼ cups
Chopped fresh basil and parsley	30 ml	2 tbsp	2 tbsp

① Cut the lamb and bacon into strips the same thickness as the fettucine. Cut the chillies into julienne strips.

② Add the fettucine to a pan of boiling water and cook for 8 minutes. Drain, rinse and drain again.

③ Heat the oil in a flameproof casserole (Dutch oven) and fry (sauté) the lamb, bacon, chillies and garlic for 3 minutes without browning. Add the onion and cook for another 4 minutes until dry, tossing and stirring all the time. Pour in the water and wine.

④ Cook in a preheated oven at 180°C/350°F/gas mark 4 for 45 minutes.

⑤ Stir in the fettucine and the cream and season to taste with salt and pepper. Return to the oven for about 15 minutes until heated through.

⑥ Sprinkle over the grated cheese and herbs before serving.

PREPARATION TIME: 30 MINUTES
COOKING TIME: 1 HOUR
CHIANTI TO ACCOMPANY

LAMB AND APRICOT CASSEROLE

For speed, this recipe uses no-soak dried apricots, but for the best flavour of all, soak dried apricots in freshly brewed tea for 6 hours before making the dish.

—— SERVES 4 ——

	METRIC	IMPERIAL	AMERICAN
Oil	30 ml	2 tbsp	2 tbsp
Shoulder of lamb, cubed	1 kg	2¼ lb	2¼ lb
No-soak dried apricots	450 g	1 lb	2¾ cups
Water or orange juice	300 ml	½ pt	1¼ cups
Salt and freshly ground black pepper			
Ground cumin	5 ml	1 tsp	1 tsp
Green chilli, seeded and sliced	1	1	1
Clear honey	30 ml	2 tbsp	2 tbsp
Mangetout (snow peas) or French (green) beans, to serve			

① Heat the oil in a flameproof casserole (Dutch oven) and sear the lamb for 8 minutes until brown all over. Add the apricots, water or orange juice, salt and pepper, ground cumin and chilli.

② Transfer to the oven and bake at 200°C/400°F/gas mark 6 for 40 minutes.

③ Stir in the honey and cook for a further 10 minutes until everything is tender and well blended.

④ Serve with mangetout or French beans.

PREPARATION TIME: 10 MINUTES PLUS SOAKING

COOKING TIME: 50 MINUTES

MUSCADET OR CHABLIS TO ACCOMPANY

RACK OF LAMB WITH MUSHROOMS

The best end of lamb is always a popular dish when pot-roasted. Most chefs cook rack of lamb for 30 minutes; cook it for 45 minutes if you like it well done. Ask the butcher to prepare the lamb for you if you wish.

—— SERVES 4 ——

	METRIC	IMPERIAL	AMERICAN
Butter or margarine	15 g	½ oz	1 tbsp
Oil	30 ml	2 tbsp	2 tbsp
Rack of lamb, trimmed and chined (spinal bones removed)	1	1	1
Medium sherry	120 ml	4 fl oz	½ cup
Water or meat stock	120 ml	4 fl oz	½ cup
Tomato purée (paste)	5 ml	1 tsp	1 tsp
Salt and freshly ground black pepper			
Field or wild mushrooms	450 g	1 lb	1 lb
Sautéed potatoes and steamed broccoli, to serve			

① Heat the butter or margarine and oil in a flameproof casserole (Dutch oven) and brown the rack of lamb for 8 minutes, then transfer into the oven without a lid. Cook for 25 minutes at 200°C/400°F/gas mark 6.

② Remove the surplus fat from the casserole, then add the sherry, water or stock, tomato purée, seasoning and mushrooms. Cover and cook for 20 minutes

③ Cut the rack into cutlets and serve with sautéed potatoes and steamed broccoli.

PREPARATION TIME: 20 MINUTES
COOKING TIME: 45 MINUTES
AUSTRALIAN CABERNET TO ACCOMPANY

CASSEROLED LAMB DUMPLINGS IN SAFFRON RICE

—— SERVES 6 ——

	METRIC	IMPERIAL	AMERICAN
Lean minced (ground) lamb	450 g	I lb	I lb
Chopped fresh mixed herbs, such as parsley, mint, and basil	45 ml	3 tbsp	3 tbsp
Fresh white breadcrumbs	30 ml	2 tbsp	2 tbsp
Eggs, beaten	2	2	2
Raisins	50 g	2 oz	⅓ cup
Green chilli, seeded and chopped (optional)	I	I	I
Onions, chopped	2	2	2
Salt and freshly ground black pepper			
Oil	90 ml	6 tbsp	6 tbsp
Long-grain rice	150 g	5 oz	¾ cup
A pinch of saffron powder			
Garlic clove, chopped	I	I	I
Water	450 ml	¾ pt	2 cups

① To make the dumplings, combine the minced lamb, herbs, breadcrumbs, eggs, raisins, chilli (if using), and 1 chopped onion. Season with salt and pepper and divide into 16 small dumplings.

② Heat half the oil in a flameproof casserole (Dutch oven) and brown the dumplings for 5 minutes. Remove and set aside.

③ For the rice, heat the remaining oil in the casserole and fry (sauté) the remaining onion until golden. Add the rice, saffron, garlic and water, bring to the boil, then simmer for 8 minutes. Season with salt and pepper and add the dumplings.

④ Cover and cook in a preheated oven at 200°C/400°F/gas mark 6 for 25–30 minutes.

PREPARATION TIME: 25 MINUTES
COOKING TIME: 25–30 MINUTES
LIGHT ROSÉ WINE TO ACCOMPANY

BEEF AND VEAL CASSEROLES

Cheaper cuts of beef are well-suited for the long, slow process of cooking in a casserole (Dutch oven), during which the meat becomes succulent and saturated with the cooking liquor. Braised or pot-roasted beef is usually tenderised further by soaking it in a marinade before cooking. Beef is also tenderised by hanging, and a good butcher will sell beef which has had a little time to mature. Another effective method is to include fruits with tenderising properties, such as fresh pineapple, figs and papaya (pawpaw) in the recipes.

Topside, top rump and silverside are also excellent joints for pot-roasting and braising, but because of the quality of the meat, they also tend to be more expensive. You will also see thick slices simply labelled braising steak in the supermarkets.

Cuts that are suitable for boiling and stewing are usually less expensive. Look or ask for chuck steak, brisket, shin, leg or shank. You can also buy packs of ready-diced stewing beef in the supermarket, which are fine for any casserole.

Veal is also a wonderful meat for the casserole and, being very tender, does not require as long a cooking time as beef, although a tasty sauce is needed to complement its rather bland flavour. Less expensive cuts from the forequarters are used for braising, pot-roasting and for pies.

STEAK AND KIDNEY CASSEROLE

This is an old Royal Navy favourite from the war when I served as a cook to the First Lord of the Admiralty Submarine Command. The port transforms what could otherwise be quite an ordinary stew.

—— SERVES 6 ——

	METRIC	IMPERIAL	AMERICAN
Seasoned plain (all-purpose) flour	30 ml	2 tbsp	2 tbsp
Mustard powder	15 ml	1 tbsp	1 tbsp
Chuck steak, cut into 2.5 cm/1 in cubes	1 kg	2¼ lb	2¼ lb
Ox kidney, trimmed and cut into small pieces	1	1	1
Oil	30 ml	2 tbsp	2 tbsp
Water	300 ml	½ pt	1¼ cups
Ruby port	300 ml	½ pt	1¼ cups
Onion, diced	1	1	1
Carrot, diced	1	1	1
Celery stick, diced	1	1	1
Salt and freshly ground black pepper			
A pinch of dried thyme			
Jacket or creamed potatoes, cauliflower and carrots, to serve			

① Mix the seasoned flour with the mustard and rub the mixture over the steak and kidney.

② Heat the oil in a flameproof casserole (Dutch oven) and fry (sauté) the meat until browned. Add the water, half the port and all the remaining ingredients except the thyme.

③ Transfer to the oven and braise at 180°C/350°F/gas mark 4 for 1¼ hours.

④ Add the remaining port and a pinch of thyme. Cover and cook for a further 15 minutes.

PREPARATION TIME: 20 MINUTES
COOKING TIME: 1½ HOURS
SPANISH RED WINE, SUCH AS RIOJA, TO ACCOMPANY

RICH BEEF STEW

This recipe is based on a rich Parisian dish famed in France for its succulence. The meat is taken from the rump and should be cut about 1 cm/½ in thick.

—— SERVES 4 ——

	METRIC	IMPERIAL	AMERICAN
Braising steaks, about 225 g/8 oz each	4	4	4
Seasoned plain (all-purpose) flour	50 g	2 oz	¼ cup
Oil	45 ml	3 tbsp	3 tbsp
Madeira	150 ml	¼ pt	¾ cup
Beef stock	300 ml	½ pt	1¼ cups
Button mushrooms	450 g	1 lb	1 lb
Button (pearl) onions	450 g	1 lb	1 lb
Stuffed olives	225 g	8 oz	1½ cups
Clear honey	5 ml	1 tsp	1 tsp
Garlic clove, crushed	1	1	1
Tomato purée (paste)	15 ml	1 tbsp	1 tbsp
Dried tarragon	2.5 ml	½ tsp	½ tsp
Salt and freshly ground black pepper			
French (green) beans or flageolets, to serve			

① Coat the steaks in the seasoned flour and shake off the surplus.

② Heat the oil in a casserole (Dutch oven) and fry (sauté) the steaks for 3 minutes on each side until browned. Remove the surplus oil and add all the remaining ingredients. Bring to the boil.

③ Transfer to the oven and bake at 180°C/350°F/gas mark 4 for 1¾–2 hours until very tender. Add a little more water or Madeira during cooking as necessary to keep the meat bathed in sauce. Serve with French beans or flageolets.

PREPARATION TIME: 15 MINUTES
COOKING TIME: 1¾–2 HOURS
BEAUJOLAIS OR VERY DRY MADEIRA WINE TO ACCOMPANY

GERMAN-STYLE BEEFBURGER CASSEROLE

Beefburgers are probably tastiest when cooked in their own juices. The burgers in this receipe are highly seasoned and enriched with eggs and fresh herbs.

—— SERVES 4–8 ——

	METRIC	IMPERIAL	AMERICAN
Lean minced (ground) beef	I kg	2¼ lb	2¼ lb
Onion, chopped	I	I	I
Egg, beaten	I	I	I
Chopped fresh parsley	45 ml	3 tbsp	3 tbsp
Caraway seeds (optional)	5 ml	I tsp	I tsp
Fresh white breadcrumbs	50 g	2 oz	I cup
Salt and freshly ground black pepper			
Oil	45 ml	3 tbsp	3 tbsp
Carrots, very thinly sliced	450 g	I lb	I lb
Onion, sliced	I	I	I
Celery stick, sliced	I	I	I
Strong brown German beer	300 ml	½ pt	I ¼ cups
Water	300 ml	½ pt	I ¼ cups
Clear honey	5 ml	I tsp	I tsp
A pinch of ground mace			

① Combine the minced beef, onion, egg, parsley, caraway seeds, if using, breadcrumbs and seasoning, then shape into eight balls and flatten slightly to about 2.5 cm/1 in thick.

② Heat the oil in a flameproof casserole (Dutch oven) and brown the burgers for 5 minutes. Discard the surplus oil. Add the carrots, onion, celery, beer, water and honey, and season with salt, pepper and mace.

③ Cover and gently braise in a preheated oven at 180°C/ 350°F/gas mark 4 for 1 hour.

PREPARATION TIME: 30 MINUTES

COOKING TIME: 1 HOUR

STRONG BROWN GERMAN BEER IS IDEAL, OR LAGER IF YOU PREFER

BEEF AND BRAMLEY CASSEROLE

Apple and beef make a good combination, contrasting in taste and texture with the cabbage and other ingredients in this dish. It is important to sear the meat well to enhance the beefy taste.

—— SERVES 4 ——

	METRIC	IMPERIAL	AMERICAN
Topside braising steaks	4	4	4
Seasoned plain (all-purpose) flour	50 g	2 oz	½ cup
Oil	45 ml	3 tbsp	3 tbsp
Green cabbage, shredded	½	½	½
Large cooking (tart) apples, cored and sliced	4	4	4
Onion, thinly sliced	I	I	I
Water or dry cider	300 ml	½ pt	I ¼ cups
Salt and freshly ground black pepper			
Light brown sugar	I5 ml	I tbsp	I tbsp
Caraway seeds	5 ml	I tsp	I tsp

① Coat the steak with the seasoned flour and shake off the surplus.

② Heat the oil in a flameproof casserole (Dutch oven) and fry (sauté) the meat for 5 minutes until brown on both sides. Remove the surplus oil.

③ Add the cabbage, apples, onion and water or cider. Bring to the boil, then season with salt, pepper and sugar and add the caraway seeds. Cover and braise in a preheated oven at 180°C/350°F/gas mark 4 for 1½ hours.

PREPARATION TIME: 20 MINUTES

COOKING TIME: 1½ HOURS

CIDER TO ACCOMPANY

MEAT LOAF WITH LEEKS

This is a very cheap yet tender beef dish.

—— SERVES 4–6 ——

	METRIC	IMPERIAL	AMERICAN
Minced (ground) beef	I kg	2¼ lb	2¼ lb
Egg, beaten	I	I	I
White breadcrumbs	50 g	2 oz	I cup
Chopped fresh parsley, basil and chives, mixed	30 ml	2 tbsp	2 tbsp
Salt	5 ml	I tsp	I tsp
Freshly ground black pepper	1.5 ml	¼ tsp	¼ tsp
Oil	45 ml	3 tbsp	3 tbsp
Butter or margarine	15 g	½ oz	I tbsp
Leeks, white part only, sliced	3	3	3
Dry white wine	300 ml	½ pt	1¼ cups

① Blend the minced beef with the egg, breadcrumbs and herbs and season with salt and pepper. Put the mixture on a floured board and shape into a thick roll about 6 cm/2½ in in diameter.

② Heat the oil and butter or margarine in a flameproof casserole (Dutch oven) and add the leeks. Put the meat roll on top of the layer of leeks, pour over the wine and season with salt and pepper.

③ Braise, uncovered, in a preheated oven at 200°C/400°F/gas mark 6 for 45 minutes until the meat loaf is lightly browned, basting with wine from time to time.

④ Serve cut into four thick slices.

PREPARATION TIME: 15 MINUTES
COOKING TIME: 45 MINUTES
DRY CIDER OR LAGER TO ACCOMPANY

CHINESE BEEF WITH ALMONDS
—— SERVES 4–6 ——

	METRIC	IMPERIAL	AMERICAN
Thick beef flank	I kg	2¼ lb	2¼ lb
Pineapple juice	150 ml	¼ pt	⅔ cup
Clear honey	15 ml	I tbsp	I tbsp
Soy sauce	15 ml	I tbsp	I tbsp
Piece of fresh root ginger, peeled	2.5 cm	I in	I in
Garlic clove	I	I	I
Onion	I	I	I
Oil	10 ml	2 tsp	2 tsp
Sherry vinegar	15 ml	I tbsp	I tbsp
Salt and freshly ground black pepper			
A pinch of five-spice powder			
Small chilli, seeded and chopped	I	I	I
Cornflour (cornstarch)	5 ml	I tsp	I tsp
Water	300 ml	½ pt	1¼ cups
Blanched almonds	100 g	4 oz	I cup
Noodles or spaghetti, to serve			

① Cut the meat into very thin strips 4 cm/1½ in long.

② Liquidise all the remaining ingredients except the cornflour, water and almonds and pour into a casserole (Dutch oven). Add the meat, cover and chill for 2 hours.

③ Blend the cornflour and water and season with salt and pepper. Stir into the casserole. Braise in a preheated oven at 180°C/350°F/gas mark 4 for 20 minutes.

④ Stir the casserole well, taste and adjust the seasoning if necessary. Continue braising for a further 30 minutes, adding a little water if the liquid evaporates too quickly.

⑤ Add the almonds and continue to cook for a further 10 minutes until the meat is very tender. Serve with noodles or spaghetti.

PREPARATION TIME: 15 MINUTES PLUS MARINATING
COOKING TIME: 1 HOUR
SAKE OR A LIGHT, FRUITY WHITE WINE TO ACCOMPANY

BEEF IN RED WINE
—— SERVES 4–6 ——

	METRIC	IMPERIAL	AMERICAN
Oil	45 ml	3 tbsp	3 tbsp
Silverside or boned rib joint	1 kg	2¼ lb	2¼ lb
Red wine	300 ml	½ pt	1¼ cups
Beef stock	300 ml	½ pt	1¼ cups
Tomato purée (paste)	45 ml	3 tbsp	3 tbsp
A sprig of thyme			
Small onions	8	8	8
Small carrots	8	8	8
Salt and freshly ground black pepper			
Cornflour (cornstarch)	5 ml	1 tsp	1 tsp
Cold water	120 ml	4 fl oz	½ cup
Green vegetables, to serve			

① Heat the oil in a flameproof casserole (Dutch oven) and brown the meat all over for 6 minutes. Remove the surplus oil and transfer to a preheated oven at 200°C/400°F/gas mark 6 and cook for 30 minutes.

② Reduce the oven temperature to 180°C/350°F/gas mark 4. Add the wine, beef stock, tomato purée, thyme, onions and carrots and season with salt and pepper. Cover and cook gently for 1½ hours. During cooking, maintain the level of liquid by adding a little more water as necessary. Turn the joint over once or twice.

③ Remove the meat, onions and carrots from the casserole and keep them warm. Blend together the cornflour and water and stir into the casserole. Bring to the boil, stirring until thickened and glossy. Season the sauce and remove the thyme.

④ To serve, carve the meat into thin slices and accompany with the onions and carrots and green vegetables.

PREPARATION TIME: 15 MINUTES
COOKING TIME: 2 HOURS
BULGARIAN RED OR AUSTRALIAN CABERNET TO ACCOMPANY

STEAK CASSEROLE WITH BEANS

This hot-pot casserole is as old as the Incas and is still often served in Latin American countries.

—— SERVES 4 ——

	METRIC	IMPERIAL	AMERICAN
Dried haricot (navy) beans, soaked overnight in water	225 g	8 oz	2 cups
Carrots, peeled and trimmed	4	4	4
Onions, chopped	4	4	4
Celery stick	I	I	I
Water	I litre	1¾ pts	4¼ cups
A sprig of thyme			
Beef skirt, cut into small steaks	I kg	2¼ lb	2¼ lb
Salt and freshly ground black pepper			
Pickled gherkins (cornichons), chutney and beetroot (red beet) salad, to serve			

① Drain the beans, then place in a flameproof casserole (Dutch oven) with the carrots, onions, celery and water. Bring the liquid to the boil and remove the scum as it rises. Boil rapidly for 10 minutes. Add the thyme.

② Place the beef on top of the beans and season with pepper only. Cover and braise in a preheated oven at 180°C/350°F/ gas mark 4 for 2¼ hours. Check and adjust the liquid level during cooking. Add salt to taste at the last minute.

③ Serve hot with pickled gherkins, chutney and a beetroot salad.

PREPARATION TIME: 15 MINUTES PLUS SOAKING
COOKING TIME: 2¼ HOURS
RED OR ROSÉ WINE FROM PROVENCE TO ACCOMPANY

FRENCH BEEF OLIVES
—— SERVES 8 ——

	METRIC	IMPERIAL	AMERICAN
Pork sausagemeat	450 g	I lb	I lb
Chopped fresh parsley	30 ml	2 tbsp	2 tbsp
Stoned (pitted) green olives, chopped	30 ml	2 tbsp	2 tbsp
Egg, beaten	I	I	I
Plain (all-purpose) flour	30 ml	2 tbsp	2 tbsp
Thin steaks, about 225 g/8 oz each	8	8	8
Oil	30 ml	2 tbsp	2 tbsp
Carrots, sliced	4	4	4
Small turnips, sliced	4	4	4
Red wine	300 ml	½ pt	1¼ cups
Tomato purée (paste)	30 ml	2 tbsp	2 tbsp
Salt and freshly ground black pepper			
Cornflour (cornstarch)	15 ml	I tbsp	I tbsp

1. Mix together the sausagemeat, parsley, olives, egg and flour and divide into eight portions.

2. Beat the steaks with a wooden mallet until thin and wide. Place a portion of filling on each steak and wrap it to make an oval shape. Tie with cooks' string.

3. Heat the oil in a flameproof casserole (Dutch oven) and brown the beef olives for 8 minutes. Lift out, then add the carrots and turnips and place the beef olives on top. Pour over the wine, just enough water to cover and add the tomato purée. Season with salt and pepper.

4. Cover and braise in a preheated oven at 180°C/350°F/gas mark 4 for 1½ hours. Remove the string and keep warm.

5. Blend the cornflour with a little water. Stir into the casserole, bring to the boil, then simmer for 2 minutes, stirring until thickened and clear. Season to taste with salt and pepper and serve separately with the beef olives.

PREPARATION TIME: 30 MINUTES
COOKING TIME: 1½ HOURS
BEAUJOLAIS OR MACON TO ACCOMPANY

BEEF IN BEER

This dish originated in Belgium and has become popular in countries where beer is a national drink. Guinness and dark German stouts give the best flavour.

—— SERVES 6 ——

	METRIC	IMPERIAL	AMERICAN
Topside or silverside of beef	1.5 kg	3 lb	3 lb
Seasoned plain (all-purpose) flour	50 g	2 oz	½ cup
Oil	60 ml	4 tbsp	4 tbsp
Onions, sliced	450 g	1 lb	1 lb
Dark stout or Guinness	600 ml	1 pt	2½ cups
Malt vinegar	15 ml	1 tbsp	1 tbsp
Light brown sugar or clear honey	25 g	1 oz	2 tbsp
Water	300 ml	½ pt	1¼ cups
A sprig of thyme			
Celery stick, chopped	1	1	1
Salt and freshly ground black pepper			
Ground mace	2.5 ml	½ tsp	½ tsp

①   Cut the meat into six large, thick slices. Coat in the seasoned flour.

②   Heat half the oil in a flameproof casserole (Dutch oven) and fry (sauté) the steaks for 2 minutes on each side. Remove from the dish.

③   Add the remaining oil and fry the onions for 2 minutes. Pour in the stout or Guinness, malt vinegar, sugar or honey and water and boil for 2 minutes. Add the meat with the thyme and celery. Season with the salt, pepper and ground mace.

④   Cover and braise in a preheated oven at 180°C/350°F/gas mark 4 for 1½ hours.

PREPARATION TIME: 15 MINUTES
COOKING TIME: 1½ HOURS
BEER, ALE OR STOUT TO ACCOMPANY

HUNGARIAN BEEF GOULASH

Traditionally the potatoes are cooked separately and added just before serving, but for speed, you can cook them in the goulash.

—— SERVES 6 ——

	METRIC	IMPERIAL	AMERICAN
Plain (all-purpose) flour	50 g	2 oz	½ cup
Mild paprika	15 ml	I tbsp	I tbsp
Flank of beef, cut into 2.5 cm/I in cubes	1.5 kg	3 lb	3 lb
Oil	60 ml	4 tbsp	4 tbsp
Onion, sliced	150 g	5 oz	5 oz
Water	600 ml	I pt	2½ cups
Tomato purée (paste)	15 ml	I tbsp	I tbsp
Ground allspice	2.5 ml	½ tsp	½ tsp
Salt	5 ml	I tsp	I tsp
Small new potatoes, scrubbed	450 g	I lb	I lb
Chopped fresh parsley	30 ml	2 tbsp	2 tbsp

① Sift the flour and paprika together and use to coat the beef.

② Heat the oil in a flameproof casserole (Dutch oven) and brown the meat for 5 minutes. Add the onion and cook for 2 minutes. Blend in the water, tomato purée, allspice and salt. Add the potatoes.

③ Cover and bake in a preheated oven at 180°C/350°F/gas mark 4 for 1½ hours. Check and adjust the liquid level if necessary.

④ Sprinkle with parsley before serving.

PREPARATION TIME: 15 MINUTES
COOKING TIME: 1½ HOURS
A ROBUST HUNGARIAN RED WINE TO ACCOMPANY

POACHED BEEF WITH VEGETABLES

This is my version of the classic French dish, Boeuf à la Mode. It is delicious served hot or cold. You will need to tie up the joint with cooks' string before cooking.

—— SERVES 6 ——

	METRIC	IMPERIAL	AMERICAN
Oil	60 ml	4 tbsp	4 tbsp
Whole piece of topside	1.5 kg	3 lb	3 lb
Calves' feet, split (optional)	2	2	2
Carrot, unpeeled, cut into chunks	1	1	1
Leek, white part only, trimmed	1	1	1
Onion, quartered	1	1	1
Dry white wine	300 ml	½ pt	1¼ cups
A piece of bacon rind			
Beef stock cubes, crumbled	2	2	2
Water	600 ml	1 pt	2½ cups
Celery stick, sliced	1	1	1
Garlic cloves, chopped	2	2	2
Tomato purée (paste)	15 ml	1 tbsp	1 tbsp
A small bunch of fresh tarragon			
Cornflour (cornstarch)	15 ml	1 tbsp	1 tbsp
Water	45 ml	3 tbsp	3 tbsp
Salt and freshly ground black pepper			
Carrots, cut into sticks	2	2	2
Turnips, cut into sticks	2	2	2
French (green) beans, trimmed and cut to equal size	225 g	8 oz	8 oz
Butter	100 g	4 oz	½ cup
Chopped fresh parsley	30 ml	2 tbsp	2 tbsp
French dressing or mayonnaise and lettuce leaves, to serve			

①   Heat the oil in a flameproof casserole (Dutch oven) and brown the joint and calves' feet, if using, all over for 15 minutes.

②   Remove the joint and feet and brown the carrot, leek and onion for 5 minutes. Return the meat and calves' feet to the dish and add the wine and bacon rind. Crumble in a stock cube, add the water and bring to the boil.

③   Cover, transfer to a preheated oven and cook at 180°C/350°F/gas mark 4 for 2 hours.

④   Transfer the joint to a dish and discard the string. Discard the bones from the calves' feet and dice the meat.

⑤   Strain the cooking juices into a measuring jug and add 600 ml/1 pt/2½ cups to the casserole. Add the celery, garlic, tomato purée and tarragon and boil for 5 minutes

⑥   Blend together the cornflour and water with a cupful of the sauce and add to the saucepan. Cook for a further 4 minutes. Strain and season with salt and pepper.

⑦   Boil the carrots, turnips and French beans in salted water for 10 minutes, then rinse in hot water.

⑧   If serving hot, carve the meat thinly and serve with the diced calves' feet meat and the vegetables garnished with butter and parsley. Some people like it with French dressing.

⑨   If the meat is to be served cold, simply put it in a deep dish and cover completely with the sauce, which will form a jelly on cooling. Mix the vegetables in mayonnaise and serve with lettuce leaves.

PREPARATION TIME: 35 MINUTES

COOKING TIME: 2 HOURS

ROSÉ OR PROVENÇAL RED WINE TO ACCOMPANY

AUSTRIAN BEEF CASSEROLE WITH HORSERADISH SAUCE

—— SERVES 6 ——

	METRIC	IMPERIAL	AMERICAN
Oil	50 ml	2 fl oz	3½ tbsp
Stewing beef, cubed	1 kg	2¼ lb	2¼ lb
Onions, sliced	6	6	6
Water	1.5 litres	2½ pts	6 cups
Beef stock cubes, crumbled	3	3	3
Bouquet garni sachet	1	1	1
Leeks	6	6	6
Water	150 ml	¼ pt	⅔ cup
White vinegar	25 ml	1½ tbsp	1½ tbsp
Horseradish, scraped	175 g	6 oz	6 oz
Cooking (tart) apples, peeled and cored	175 g	6 oz	6 oz
Fresh white breadcrumbs	25 g	1 oz	½ cup
Single (light) cream	50 ml	2 fl oz	3½ tbsp

①   Heat the oil in a flameproof casserole (Dutch oven) and brown the meat, covered with a lid, for 8 minutes, stirring frequently. Add the onions and brown for 3 minutes. Cover with the water mixed with the stock cubes and bouquet garni sachet.

②   Wash the leeks, cut into four lengthways, tie in a bundle and put into the casserole with the meat. Bring to the boil, and remove the scum as it rises to the surface. Simmer for 2–2½ hours or braise in a preheated oven at 160°C/325°F/ gas mark 3 until the meat is tender.

③   Meanwhile, put the water and vinegar in a bowl and grate in the horseradish and apple. Soak for 1 hour. Drain off the liquid and mix the breadcrumbs and cream into the mixture. Place in a serving bowl.

④   When the meat is cooked, strain off the broth. Remove the string from the leeks and serve on top of the meat.

PREPARATION TIME: 30 MINUTES
COOKING TIME: 2½ HOURS
CRISP AUSTRIAN WHITE WINE TO ACCOMPANY

CASSEROLE OF BEEF SAUSAGES IN PEANUT SAUCE

This economical and delicious dish is best made with fresh sausages bought from your butcher.

—— SERVES 4 ——

	METRIC	IMPERIAL	AMERICAN
Oil	30 ml	2 tbsp	2 tbsp
Large beef sausages	8	8	8
Salted peanuts, ground to a powder	100 g	4 oz	1 cup
Tomato ketchup (catsup)	15 ml	1 tbsp	1 tbsp
Yeast extract	5 ml	1 tsp	1 tsp
Water	300 ml	½ pt	1¼ cups
Juice of 1 orange			
Salt and freshly ground black pepper			

① Heat the oil in a flameproof casserole (Dutch oven) and brown the sausages all over for 4 minutes. Remove the surplus oil.

② Stir in all the remaining ingredients.

③ Cover and braise in a preheated oven at 200°C/400°F/gas mark 6 for 12 minutes.

PREPARATION TIME: 5 MINUTES
COOKING TIME: 12 MINUTES
MUSCADET OR BEAUJOLAIS TO ACCOMPANY

PEANUT AND BEEF CASSEROLE

Peanuts are an excellent source of protein. For this dish use fresh, shelled peanuts, crushed or coarsely chopped. Roasting them a little enhances the flavour. The stew can be served hot, or cold with lettuce leaves as a sandwich filler.

—— SERVES 4 ——

	METRIC	IMPERIAL	AMERICAN
Peanut oil	60 ml	4 tbsp	4 tbsp
Onion, chopped	I	I	I
Green chilli, seeded and chopped	I	I	I
Shin of beef, cut into 1 cm/½ in cubes	450 g	I lb	I lb
Tomato purée (paste)	15 ml	I tbsp	I tbsp
Pulp and juice of I fresh fig			
Peanuts, ground	150 g	5 oz	I¼ cups
Water	600 ml	I pt	2½ cups
Salt and freshly ground black pepper			
Chopped fresh root ginger	5 ml	I tsp	I tsp
Green bananas, peeled and sliced	2	2	2
Chopped fresh basil	30 ml	2 tbsp	2 tbsp
Boiled rice, to serve			

① Heat the oil in a flameproof casserole (Dutch oven) and fry (sauté) the onions, chilli and beef for 8 minutes. Add the tomato purée, fig pulp and juice, peanuts and water, and season with salt and pepper. Bring to the boil.

② Cover and simmer on a low heat on top of the stove for 1½ hours. Check and adjust the level of liquid during cooking. Add the ginger halfway through cooking.

③ A few minutes before the dish is ready, add the bananas, season to taste with salt and pepper and sprinkle with chopped basil.

④ Serve with boiled rice.

PREPARATION TIME: 20 MINUTES
COOKING TIME: 1½ HOURS
RED BORDEAUX TO ACCOMPANY

STUFFED VEAL BREAST
—— SERVES 8 ——

	METRIC	IMPERIAL	AMERICAN
Breast of veal	2 kg	4½ lb	4½ lb
For the stuffing:			
Cooked long-grain rice	100 g	4 oz	1 cup
Beef sausagemeat	100 g	4 oz	4 oz
Onion, chopped	1	1	1
Chopped fresh parsley	30 ml	2 tbsp	2 tbsp
Eggs	2	2	2
Salt and freshly ground black pepper			
For the gravy:			
Oil	45 ml	3 tbsp	3 tbsp
Carrot, chopped	1	1	1
Onion, chopped	1	1	1
Celery stick, chopped	1	1	1
Water	600 ml	1 pt	2½ cups
Stock cubes, crumbled	2	2	2
Cornflour (cornstarch)	15 ml	1 tbsp	1 tbsp
Water	45 ml	3 tbsp	3 tbsp

①   Open the cavity in the breast of veal. Combine all the stuffing ingredients and fill the pocket. Sew up with cooks' string and season with salt and pepper.

②   Heat the oil in a flameproof casserole (Dutch oven) and brown the meat all over for 15 minutes. Add the carrot, onion and celery. Add the water and the stock cubes.

③   Cover and braise in a preheated oven at 180°C/350°F/gas mark 4 for 2½ hours.

④   Remove the joint and vegetables. Blend the cornflour and water, stir into the gravy and boil for 4 minutes on top of the cooker. Season to taste and strain.

PREPARATION TIME: 30 MINUTES
COOKING TIME: 2½ HOURS
MUSCADET OR SANCERRE WINE TO ACCOMPANY

VEAL WITH GARLIC SAUCE

—— SERVES 4–6 ——

	METRIC	IMPERIAL	AMERICAN
Oil	25 ml	1½ tbsp	1½ tbsp
Butter or margarine	25 g	1 oz	2 tbsp
Stewing veal, cut into 1 cm/½ in cubes	1.5 kg	3 lb	3 lb
Onion, chopped	1	1	1
Veal stock	300 ml	½ pt	1¼ cups
Dry Madeira	120 ml	4 fl oz	½ cup
Salt and freshly ground black pepper			
A pinch of paprika			
A pinch of chilli powder			
Garlic bulb, unpeeled	1	1	1
Egg yolk	1	1	1
Single (light) cream	120 ml	4 fl oz	½ cup
Cornflour (cornstarch)	5 ml	1 tsp	1 tsp
Pasta shells or rice, to serve			

① Heat the oil and butter or margarine in a flameproof casserole (Dutch oven) and brown the veal and onion for 5 minutes, stirring occasionally. Add the veal stock, Madeira, seasoning, paprika and chilli powder.

② Divide the garlic bulb and boil the cloves in water for 10 minutes. Peel and pulp the garlic cloves and add to the veal. Simmer for 1½ hours.

③ In a cup, blend the egg yolk, cream and cornflour. Stir a little of the veal stock into this mixture, then add it all to the casserole. Check and adjust the seasoning and simmer for a further 15 minutes.

④ Serve with pasta shells or rice.

PREPARATION TIME: 30 MINUTES

COOKING TIME: 1¾ HOURS

MUSCADET OR CRISP, DRY WHITE WINE TO ACCOMPANY

BRAISED VEAL WITH BRANDY

This fragrant dish is particularly good for a dinner party.

—— SERVES 4–6 ——

	METRIC	IMPERIAL	AMERICAN
A pinch of paprika			
Ground cinnamon	2.5 ml	½ tsp	½ tsp
Salt and freshly ground black pepper			
Roasting veal from leg	1.25 kg	2 lb	2 lb
Oil	30 ml	2 tbsp	2 tbsp
Butter or margarine	25 g	1 oz	2 tbsp
Small onions	6	6	6
Small carrots	6	6	6
Water	1 litre	1¾ pts	4¼ cups
Double (heavy) cream	120 ml	4 fl oz	½ cup
Cornflour (cornstarch)	15 ml	1 tbsp	1 tbsp
Water	75 ml	5 tbsp	5 tbsp
Brandy	50 ml	2 fl oz	3½ tbsp
Chopped fresh mint	30 ml	2 tbsp	2 tbsp
Rice or new potatoes, to serve			

① Rub the paprika, cinnamon and seasoning all over the veal. Heat the oil and butter or margarine in a flameproof casserole (Dutch oven) and brown all over for 15 minutes. Add the onions, carrots and water.

② Cover and braise in a preheated oven at 180°C/350°F/gas mark 4 for 1½ hours.

③ Remove the joint and vegetables. Place the casserole on top of the stove and add the cream. Bring to the boil.

④ Blend the cornflour and water, then add them to the sauce, whisking continuously. Bring to the boil. Check and adjust the seasoning. Add the brandy and sprinkle in the chopped mint. Slice the veal and coat it with sauce.

⑤ Serve with rice or new potatoes.

PREPARATION TIME: 25 MINUTES
COOKING TIME: 1½ HOURS
SANCERRE OR WHITE MACON TO ACCOMPANY

SAUTÉED VEAL IN TOMATO SAUCE

This dish is equally good made with lean lamb.

—— SERVES 6 ——

	METRIC	IMPERIAL	AMERICAN
Oil	60 ml	4 tbsp	4 tbsp
Shoulder of veal, cut into 2.5 cm/1 in cubes	1 kg	2¼ lb	2¼ lb
Onion, chopped	1	1	1
Garlic cloves, chopped	3	3	3
Plain (all-purpose) flour	45 ml	3 tbsp	3 tbsp
Dry white wine	300 ml	½ pt	1¼ cups
Water	600 ml	1 pt	2½ cups
Large tomatoes, skinned, seeded and chopped	4	4	4
Tomato purée (paste)	15 ml	1 tbsp	1 tbsp
Sugar	2.5 ml	½ tsp	½ tsp
Salt and freshly ground black pepper			
Chopped fresh tarragon	15 ml	1 tbsp	1 tbsp
Rice, pasta or new potatoes, to serve			

① Heat the oil in a flameproof casserole (Dutch oven) and brown the meat for 15 minutes.

② Add the onion and garlic and toss for 2 minutes. Sprinkle in the flour and add the wine, water, tomatoes, tomato purée, sugar, seasoning and tarragon. Boil for 5 minutes, and braise in a preheated oven at 180°C/350°F/gas mark 4 for 1½ hours, adding a little water or wine as necessary to maintain the liquid level. Check and adjust the seasoning to taste.

③ Serve with rice, pasta or new potatoes.

PREPARATION TIME: 25 MINUTES
COOKING TIME: 1½ HOURS
SPANISH ROSÉ OR PROVENÇAL RED WINE TO ACCOMPANY

ITALIAN-STYLE VEAL CASSEROLE

Any cut of leg of veal can be used for this dish.

—— SERVES 6 ——

	METRIC	IMPERIAL	AMERICAN
Braising veal, diced	I kg	2¼ lb	2¼ lb
Seasoned plain (all-purpose) flour	50 g	2 oz	½ cup
Olive oil	45 ml	3 tbsp	3 tbsp
Sweet white vermouth	120 ml	4 fl oz	½ cup
Tomatoes, skinned, seeded and chopped	450 g	I lb	I lb
Water	300 ml	½ pt	1¼ cups
Onion, chopped	I	I	I
Fennel bulb, chopped	I	I	I
Chopped fresh tarragon	15 ml	I tbsp	I tbsp
Salt and freshly ground black pepper			
Peas or mangetout (snow peas), to serve			

① Coat the veal with the seasoned flour and shake off the surplus.

② Heat the oil in a flameproof casserole (Dutch oven) and brown the veal all over for 5–8 minutes. Remove the surplus oil and add the vermouth, tomatoes, water, onions, fennel and tarragon. Season to taste with salt and pepper.

③ Cover and braise in a preheated oven at 180°C/350°F/gas mark 4 for 1½ hours.

④ Serve with peas or mangetout.

PREPARATION TIME: 15 MINUTES
COOKING TIME: 1½ HOURS
WHITE CHIANTI TO ACCOMPANY

VEAL CUTLETS WITH NORMANDY SAUCE

Veal cutlets are rather large portions which are best cooked in casserole dishes. Each cutlet should be 2.5 cm/1 in thick, with the spinal bone removed.

—— SERVES 2 ——

	METRIC	IMPERIAL	AMERICAN
Oil	30 ml	2 tbsp	2 tbsp
Veal cutlets	2	2	2
Seasoned plain (all-purpose) flour	50 g	2 oz	½ cup
Eating (dessert) apples, cored, peeled and cut into wedges	2	2	2
Onion, chopped	I	I	I
Celery stick, chopped	I	I	I
Dry white wine	120 ml	4 fl oz	½ cup
Salt and freshly ground black pepper			
Double (heavy) cream	120 ml	4 fl oz	½ cup
Paprika	5 ml	I tsp	I tsp
Braised chicory (endive) or French (green) beans, to serve			

① Heat the oil in a flameproof casserole (Dutch oven). Dust the cutlets in the seasoned flour and brown for 5 minutes on each side. Remove the surplus oil and add the apple, onion, celery and white wine. Season with salt and pepper.

② Cover and braise in a preheated oven at 180°C/350°F/gas mark 4 for 45 minutes. Transfer the meat to a warm serving plate.

③ Skim the fat off the cooking liquid and blend in the cream. Season the sauce and pour over the cutlets. Sprinkle with paprika and serve with braised chicory or French beans.

PREPARATION TIME: 20 MINUTES

COOKING TIME: 45 MINUTES

MUSCADET OR OTHER CRISP, DRY WHITE WINE TO ACCOMPANY

OSSO BUCCO

—— SERVES 6 ——

	METRIC	IMPERIAL	AMERICAN
Oil	60 ml	4 tbsp	4 tbsp
Veal knuckles, cut into 2.5 cm/1 in thick rings	1.5 kg	3 lb	3 lb
Water	600 ml	1 pt	2½ cups
Dry white wine	300 ml	½ pt	1¼ cups
Juice and grated rind of 1 lemon			
Juice and grated rind of 1 orange			
Sugar	5 ml	1 tsp	1 tsp
Tomato purée (paste)	30 ml	2 tbsp	2 tbsp
Salt and freshly ground black pepper			
A sprig of thyme			
Carrots, diced	2	2	2
Turnips, diced	2	2	2
Celery sticks, diced	2	2	2
Fennel bulb, sliced	1	1	1
Garlic cloves, chopped	2	2	2
Chopped fresh parsley	30 ml	2 tbsp	2 tbsp
Rice or pasta, to serve			

① Heat the oil in a large flameproof casserole (Dutch oven) and brown the meat for 15 minutes. Add the water, wine, juice and grated rind of the lemon and the orange, sugar and tomato purée.

② Cover and stew gently for 1½ hours.

③ Season to taste with salt and pepper and add the thyme and vegetables. Cover and continue to cook for 45 minutes.

④ Transfer the meat to a warm serving plate and sprinkle with the parsley. Strain the sauce and serve the vegetables and sauce separately.

⑤ Serve with rice or pasta.

PREPARATION TIME: 30 MINUTES
COOKING TIME: 2¼ HOURS
CHIANTI CLASSICO IS THE IDEAL ACCOMPANIMENT

PORK AND BACON CASSEROLES

Pork and bacon make wonderfully flavoursome casseroles. The best cuts of pork to use are neck end of loin, shoulder, knuckle, belly and hand. You can also buy ready-diced casserole pork in supermarkets.

Any joint of bacon is suitable for casseroling but pieces of collar and hock are cheaper than back or gammon. Most recipes recommend green (unsmoked) joints, but use smoked if you prefer.

High-quality pork can be easily identified by its finely grained, firm but not flabby flesh. The shoulder cuts in particular should be marbled with whiter fat, and the skin smooth and free from wrinkles. Bacon should be a good pink colour with white fat. The rind should be thin and elastic. Avoid any cuts which appear sticky or have a strong smell.

Because of the high fat content of pork and bacon, cooking the meat with acid fruits, particularly apples and fresh pineapple, helps to tenderise the meat as well as complement the flavour. It is also worth trimming the meat well before cooking. Make sure you also remove the maximum amount of surface fat as the cooking progresses, so that the sauce or gravy will not be too greasy.

BOSTON BEAN CASSEROLE

The dried haricot (navy) beans in this recipe must be soaked overnight, then boiled in fresh water for 2 hours. Alternatively, use canned beans.

—— SERVES 6 ——

	METRIC	IMPERIAL	AMERICAN
Belly of pork, boned and rolled	I kg	2¼ lb	2¼ lb
Salt and freshly ground black pepper			
Light brown sugar	25 g	I oz	2 tbsp
Mustard powder	5 ml	I tsp	I tsp
Stock or water	600 ml	I pt	2½ cups
Celery sticks, sliced diagonally	2	2	2
Carrots, thickly sliced	2	2	2
Haricot beans (see note above)	225 g	8 oz	2 cups
Crusty bread and a tossed green salad, to serve			

① Rub the pork with the salt, pepper, sugar and mustard. Put the meat in a casserole (Dutch oven) with half the stock or water and the celery. Cover and braise in a preheated oven at 180°C/350°F/gas mark 4 for 2 hours.

② Add the carrots and haricot beans and the remaining water or stock. Continue cooking for another 40 minutes.

③ Uncover and cook for 10 more minutes to crisp the skin.

④ Serve with crusty bread and a tossed green salad

PREPARATION TIME: 15 MINUTES PLUS SOAKING AND COOKING BEANS
COOKING TIME: 3 HOURS
CHABLIS OR HOCK TO ACCOMPANY

PORK WITH APPLES

The tart apples and spices offset the richness of the pork beautifully.

—— SERVES 6 ——

	METRIC	IMPERIAL	AMERICAN
Ground cinnamon	2.5 ml	½ tsp	½ tsp
Mustard powder	2.5 ml	½ tsp	½ tsp
Ground cloves	2.5 ml	½ tsp	½ tsp
Freshly ground black pepper	2.5 ml	½ tsp	½ tsp
Salt	5 ml	I tsp	I tsp
Plain (all-purpose) flour	15 ml	I tbsp	I tbsp
Loin of pork, rind and fat removed	I kg	2¼ lb	2¼ lb
Oil	30 ml	2 tbsp	2 tbsp
Onions, sliced	225 g	8 oz	8 oz
Eating (dessert) apples, peeled, cored and sliced	450 g	I lb	I lb
Sweet cider	300 ml	½ pt	I¼ cups
Stock cube	I	I	I

① Blend together the spices, seasoning and flour and rub all over the meat.

② Heat the oil in a flameproof casserole (Dutch oven) and brown the meat all over for 15 minutes. Add the onions, apples, cider and stock cube.

③ Cover and pot-roast in a preheated oven at 180°C/350°F/ gas mark 4 for 2 hours, basting with more cider from time to time to keep the liquid level constant.

PREPARATION TIME: 25 MINUTES
COOKING TIME: 2 HOURS
MUSCADET OR CHABLIS TO ACCOMPANY

PORK CUTLETS WITH HERBS

This dish is best cooked, left to chill overnight and then reheated and served the following day.

—— SERVES 4 ——

	METRIC	IMPERIAL	AMERICAN
Best end neck cutlets, about 225 g/8 oz each	4	4	4
Seasoned plain (all-purpose) flour	30 ml	2 tbsp	2 tbsp
Oil	30 ml	2 tbsp	2 tbsp
Tomatoes, skinned, seeded and chopped	2	2	2
Green chilli, seeded and chopped	1	1	1
Dry white wine	300 ml	½ pt	1¼ cups
Chopped mixed fresh herbs, such as basil, parsley, chives, and tarragon	60 ml	4 tbsp	4 tbsp
Noodles, to serve			

① Trim the cutlets of rind and fat and coat in the seasoned flour. Heat the oil in a flameproof casserole (Dutch oven) and fry (sauté) the cutlets for 4 minutes on each side until browned. Add the tomatoes, chilli, wine and herbs.

② Cover and cook in a preheated oven at 180°C/350°F/gas mark 4 for 1 hour, adding a little more wine during cooking to keep the liquid level constant.

③ Cool, then chill overnight and reheat the next day.

④ Serve with noodles.

PREPARATION TIME: 10 MINUTES
COOKING TIME: 1 HOUR
GERMAN HOCK TO ACCOMPANY

BACON WITH GREEN CABBAGE

This traditional Irish dish has lots of flavour.

—— SERVES 8 ——

	METRIC	IMPERIAL	AMERICAN
Piece of green lean back bacon, soaked overnight	I kg	2¼ lb	2¼ lb
Black peppercorns, crushed	6	6	6
Green cabbage, cored and quartered	I	I	I
Boiled new potatoes, to serve			

① Place the bacon in a flameproof casserole (Dutch oven) and cover with cold water. Add the crushed peppercorns. Bring to the boil and simmer gently for 1½ hours.

② Add the green cabbage and cook for a further 30 minutes.

③ Serve with boiled new potatoes.

PREPARATION TIME: 5 MINUTES PLUS SOAKING

COOKING TIME: 2 HOURS

SPARKLING WINE TO ACCOMPANY

POLISH-STYLE BRAISED GAMMON

Gammon can also be braised in dry cider, lager, dry white wine, water or fruit juices such as pineapple or orange.

—— SERVES 8 ——

	METRIC	IMPERIAL	AMERICAN
Green gammon joint, soaked overnight	I kg	2¼ lb	2¼ lb
Caraway seeds	15 ml	I tbsp	I tbsp
Light brown sugar	30 ml	2 tbsp	2 tbsp
Sweet cider	750 ml	1¼ pts	3 cups
Onion, sliced	I	I	I
Carrot, sliced	I	I	I
Celery stick, sliced	I	I	I
Hot potato salad, to serve			

①   Place the gammon in a flameproof casserole (Dutch oven) and just cover with water. Bring to the boil, then simmer over a low heat for 2 hours.

②   Drain and remove the skin from the meat.

③   Sprinkle over the caraway seeds and sugar, then add the cider, onion, carrot and celery.

④   Cover and braise in a preheated oven at 180°C/350°F/gas mark 4 for 30 minutes.

⑤   Cool in its own liquor and, when cold, serve with hot potato salad.

PREPARATION TIME: 5 MINUTES PLUS SOAKING AND COOLING

COOKING TIME: 2½ HOURS

CIDER TO ACCOMPANY

DUBLIN SAUSAGE AND BACON CODDLE

My late Irish wife, Mary, often made this Dublin casserole, which she liked to garnish with sliced black pudding (blood sausage).

—— SERVES 4 ——

	METRIC	IMPERIAL	AMERICAN
Butter or margarine	40 g	1½ oz	3 tbsp
Oil	15 ml	1 tbsp	1 tbsp
Large pork sausages	8	8	8
Thick green gammon slices	8	8	8
Onion, sliced	1	1	1
Potatoes, sliced	4	4	4
For the sauce:			
Brown beer or stout	300 ml	½ pt	1¼ cups
Yeast extract	15 ml	1 tbsp	1 tbsp
Water or beef stock	150 ml	¼ pt	⅔ cup
Salt	5 ml	1 tsp	1 tsp
Black peppercorns, crushed	6	6	6
Made mustard	5 ml	1 tsp	1 tsp
Chopped fresh parsley, to garnish			

① Heat the butter or margarine and oil in a large flameproof casserole (Dutch oven) and brown the sausages and gammon all over for 4 minutes. Add the onion and cook for a further 2 minutes. Remove the casserole from the heat and cover the meat with sliced potatoes.

② In a bowl, combine the sauce ingredients and pour over the potatoes, sausages and gammon.

③ Cover and braise in a preheated oven for 45 minutes at 180°C/350°F/gas mark 4 until the potatoes are cooked.

④ Sprinkle with parsley and serve.

PREPARATION TIME: 10 MINUTES
COOKING TIME: 45 MINUTES
STOUT TO ACCOMPANY

GARLIC SAUSAGE AND CABBAGE CASSEROLE

This tasty German recipe is quick and easy to make.

—— SERVES 4 ——

	METRIC	IMPERIAL	AMERICAN
Butter or margarine	50 g	2 oz	¼ cup
Savoy cabbage, finely shredded	225 g	8 oz	8 oz
Onion, chopped	I	I	I
Water	300 ml	½ pt	1¼ cups
Chicken stock cube	I	I	I
Caraway seeds	5 ml	I tsp	I tsp
Salt	5 ml	I tsp	I tsp
Black peppercorns, crushed	6	6	6
Gin	30 ml	2 tbsp	2 tbsp
Garlic sausage, thickly sliced	450 g	I lb	I lb
Boiled new potatoes, to serve			

① Heat the butter or margarine in a flameproof casserole (Dutch oven) and stir in the cabbage and onion for 3 minutes to develop their flavours. Add the water, stock cube, caraway seeds, salt, crushed peppercorns and gin.

② Cover and braise in a preheated oven at 200°C/400°F/gas mark 6 for 20 minutes.

③ Add the garlic sausage and heat for just 5 minutes with the lid on.

④ Serve with boiled new potatoes.

PREPARATION TIME: 10 MINUTES
COOKING TIME: 25 MINUTES
STOUT TO ACCOMPANY

VEGETABLE AND PULSE CASSEROLES

The word has spread rapidly in recent years that a good diet should contain a high proportion of fresh vegetables, cooked so that they are crisp, fresh and colourful, not soggy and overdone. With the ever-widening range of produce available in the supermarkets, there is plenty to choose from. Not only that, but we can choose from a range of international cooking styles, from the French way of serving individual vegetables such as asparagus or mangetout (snow peas) as a delicacy on their own, to the Indian – capturing a thousand fragrances in a single dish of lentils – or even the Far Eastern, where sweet and spicy are blended to perfection.

Choose fresh, crisp vegetables, and wash them well before preparation, peeling, scraping or trimming them if necessary before slicing, chopping or dicing into even-sized pieces so that they are all cooked in the same amount of time. Vegetables which tend to discolour once prepared, such as potatoes, can be soaked in water with a little lemon juice.

Dried pulses will take less time to cook if they are soaked in cold water for at least an hour beforehand. Beans and chick peas (garbanzos) must be soaked overnight and will take about 2 hours to cook either in a pan of water or in a covered casserole (Dutch oven) in a preheated oven at 180°C/350°F/ gas mark 4.

The best way to develop good flavour in a casserole is to start by frying (sautéing) the onions, garlic and root vegetables before adding the pulses or precooked beans and starchy vegetables. Leafy vegetables, herbs and spices can be added at the last minute.

BRAISED CHICORY

Cooked in lemon juice and butter, chicory (endive) is very popular as an accompaniment for veal or pork escalopes. To reduce the bitterness, cut a cone-shaped core out of the base of each head.

—— SERVES 4 ——

	METRIC	IMPERIAL	AMERICAN
Heads of white leaf chicory (Belgian endive)	8	8	8
Chicken or veal stock or water	100 ml	3½ fl oz	scant ½ cup
Butter or margarine	100 g	4 oz	½ cup
Juice of 1 lemon			
A pinch of sugar			
Salt and freshly ground black pepper			
Chopped fresh parsley	30 ml	2 tbsp	2 tbsp

① Place the chicory in a casserole (Dutch oven), cover with the stock or water and add the butter or margarine and lemon juice. Add the sugar and season to taste with salt and pepper.

② Cover and simmer gently on top of the oven for 45 minutes until tender.

③ Sprinkle with parsley just before serving.

PREPARATION TIME: 5 MINUTES
COOKING TIME: 45 MINUTES

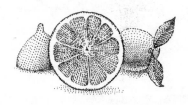

MILANESE-STYLE COURGETTES

Courgettes (zucchini) have a mild flavour, but being very watery they can be cooked in their own juice without extra liquid, and this Italian recipe is a great way to add extra flavour. If you have no saffron powder, use curry powder instead.

—— SERVES 4 ——

	METRIC	IMPERIAL	AMERICAN
Courgettes, diagonally sliced	4	4	4
Small tomatoes, skinned, seeded and chopped	4	4	4
Garlic cloves, chopped	2	2	2
Mushrooms, sliced	4	4	4
Shallot, chopped	I	I	I
Salt and freshly ground black pepper			
Celery seed	5 ml	I tsp	I tsp
A pinch of saffron powder			
Olive oil	60 ml	4 tbsp	4 tbsp
Parmesan cheese, grated, to serve			

① Place all the ingredients except the cheese in a casserole (Dutch oven).

② Cover tightly and cook in a preheated oven at 180°C/ 350°F/gas mark 4 for 20 minutes.

③ Serve with grated Parmesan cheese handed separately.

PREPARATION TIME: 10 MINUTES
COOKING TIME: 20 MINUTES

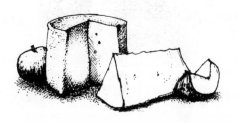

FIELD MUSHROOM AND HERB CASSEROLE

Casseroled mushrooms have a better flavour than fried (sautéed) or grilled (broiled). This particular dish, with chopped ham and a mixture of herbs, has become popular in many regions of France. It can also be eaten with fried bread or toast.

—— SERVES 4 ——

	METRIC	IMPERIAL	AMERICAN
Field or wild mushrooms, quartered	450 g	1 lb	1 lb
Olive oil	45 ml	3 tbsp	3 tbsp
Garlic cloves, chopped	3	3	3
Ham with a little fat, diced	100 g	4 oz	1 cup
Shallot, chopped	1	1	1
Chopped mixed fresh herbs, such as parsley, chives, basil and tarragon	30 ml	2 tbsp	2 tbsp
Medium sherry	120 ml	4 fl oz	½ cup

① Place all the ingredients in a casserole (Dutch oven).

② Cover and braise in a preheated oven at 200°C/400°F/gas mark 6 for 10 minutes until the mushrooms are tender.

PREPARATION TIME: 15 MINUTES
COOKING TIME: 10 MINUTES

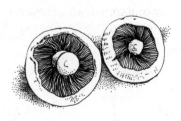

ITALIAN-STYLE FENNEL

This delicious aniseed-scented bulb is very underrated in Britain. Yet, like celery, it can be one of the most flavoursome accompaniments and makes a wonderful basis for a vegetarian main dish.

—— SERVES 4 ——

	METRIC	IMPERIAL	AMERICAN
Fennel bulbs	4	4	4
Water or stock	300 ml	½ pt	1¼ cups
Olive oil	45 ml	3 tbsp	3 tbsp
Salt and freshly ground black pepper			
Tomato, skinned, seeded and chopped	I	I	I
For the garnish:			
Parmesan cheese, grated	100 g	4 oz	I cup
Chopped fresh parsley	30 ml	2 tbsp	2 tbsp
Hard-boiled (hard-cooked) eggs, chopped (optional)	2	2	2

① Trim away the upper stems of the fennel, leaving just the bulbous roots. Set the fine, feathery leaves aside. Trim the root base, cut each fennel bulb in half lengthways, and rinse under cold water.

② Place the fennel in a casserole (Dutch oven) with the water or stock and the oil. Season with salt and pepper and cover with the chopped tomato.

③ Cover and braise in a preheated oven at 180°C/350°F/gas mark 4 for 45 minutes until tender.

④ Sprinkle over the Parmesan, parsley and chopped eggs (if using) before serving.

PREPARATION TIME: 10 MINUTES
COOKING TIME: 45 MINUTES

LONG-GRAIN RICE CASSEROLE

The rapid cooking method of this dish will help the liquid to evaporate and leave the rice grains separate. Ground turmeric makes a good substitute for the saffron powder.

—— SERVES 4 ——

	METRIC	IMPERIAL	AMERICAN
Long-grain rice	150 g	5 oz	¾ cup
Onion, chopped	I	I	I
Garlic cloves, chopped	2	2	2
Ground saffron	5 ml	I tsp	I tsp
Cooked fresh or frozen peas	100 g	4 oz	4 oz
Red (bell) pepper, seeded and diced	I	I	I
Chicken stock	600 ml	I pt	2½ cups
Butter or margarine	50 g	2 oz	¼ cup
Salt and freshly ground black pepper			

① Combine all the ingredients in a casserole (Dutch oven).

② Cover and braise in a preheated oven at 200°C/400°F/gas mark 6 for 10 minutes.

③ Stir well with a fork to separate the grains of rice, then cook for a further 10–15 minutes until the rice is just tender.

PREPARATION TIME: 10 MINUTES
COOKING TIME: 20–25 MINUTES

AUBERGINE CASSEROLE

The flavour of aubergines (eggplants) is mainly in the skin and therefore they will taste better with the skin on. To eliminate any bitter taste, you can either sprinkle salt over the cut pieces, then rinse and drain, or soak them in running water.

—— SERVES 4 ——

	METRIC	IMPERIAL	AMERICAN
Aubergines, cut into 2.5 cm/1 in cubes	2	2	2
Courgettes (zucchini), cut into 2.5 cm/1 in cubes	2	2	2
Tomatoes, skinned, seeded and diced	2	2	2
Large onion, sliced	1	1	1
Olive oil	45 ml	3 tbsp	3 tbsp
Fresh basil leaves, chopped	3	3	3
Water	300 ml	½ pt	1¼ cups
Sugar	5 ml	1 tsp	1 tsp
Salt and freshly ground black pepper			
Roasted peanuts, to garnish	100 g	4 oz	1 cup

① Put all the ingredients in a casserole (Dutch oven) and season to taste with salt and pepper.

② Cover and braise in a preheated oven at 180°C/350°F/gas mark 4 for 45 minutes until tender.

③ Garnish with the peanuts and serve hot or cold.

PREPARATION TIME: 10 MINUTES
COOKING TIME: 45 MINUTES
CHIANTI TO ACCOMPANY

BRETON HARICOT BEAN CASSEROLE

Haricot (navy) beans need soaking in water for at least 6 hours. It is best to use distilled water, because if you use hard water the insoluble minerals will cling to the beans and make them tough. If you use soda water to tenderise them they will crack open. You can treat red, black, green, flageolet and butter (lima) beans in the same way.

—— SERVES 4 ——

	METRIC	IMPERIAL	AMERICAN
Haricot beans, soaked	450 g	I lb	4 cups
Carrot, diced	I	I	I
Onion, chopped	I	I	I
Large tomatoes, skinned, seeded and chopped	2	2	2
Garlic cloves, chopped	2	2	2
A sprig of thyme			
Olive oil	30 ml	2 tbsp	2 tbsp
Water	I litre	1¾ pts	4¼ cups
Salt and freshly ground black pepper	5 ml	I tsp	I tsp

① Put all the ingredients except the seasoning in a casserole (Dutch oven).

② Cover and cook in a preheated oven at 180°C/350°F/gas mark 4 for 2 hours until tender.

③ Season with salt and pepper when cooked.

PREPARATION TIME: 10 MINUTES PLUS SOAKING
COOKING TIME: 2 HOURS

BROAD BEANS IN BUTTERMILK

Mature broad (fava) beans should be shelled, par-boiled for 6 minutes, and the tough skin of each seed removed, leaving the tender green flesh. Young, tender beans can be eaten whole.

—— SERVES 4 ——

	METRIC	IMPERIAL	AMERICAN
Broad beans, shelled	450 g	I lb	I lb
Buttermilk	120 ml	4 fl oz	½ cup
Shallot, chopped	I	I	I
Flaked (slivered) almonds	100 g	4 oz	I cup
Salt and freshly ground black pepper			

① Place all the ingredients except the seasoning in a shallow casserole (Dutch oven) but do not add salt.

② Cover and cook in a preheated oven at 200°C/400°F/gas mark 6 for 20 minutes until well blended.

③ Season with salt and pepper before serving.

PREPARATION TIME: 10 MINUTES
COOKING TIME: 20 MINUTES

CHICK PEA CASSEROLE

Chick peas (garbanzos) take 2 hours to cook even after being soaked overnight in distilled water so it is much easier to use the canned variety.

—— SERVES 4 ——

	METRIC	IMPERIAL	AMERICAN
Can of chick peas	400 g	14 oz	I large
Water	600 ml	I pt	2½ cups
Onion, chopped	I	I	I
Sesame oil	45 ml	3 tbsp	3 tbsp
A pinch of ground cumin			
Salt and freshly ground black pepper			
Spinach, shredded	150 g	5 oz	5 oz

① Put all the ingredients in a casserole (Dutch oven).

② Cover and simmer gently for 2 hours. Check after 1 hour to make sure there is enough liquid and add more water if needed. The finished casserole should be tender and well blended.

PREPARATION TIME: 5 MINUTES PLUS SOAKING
COOKING TIME: 2 HOURS

CARROT AND PARSNIP CASSEROLE

This is a dish which improves with slow cooking. The natural sugar in the root vegetables plus the honey and butter combine to give this dish its unique flavour and fragrance.

—— SERVES 4 ——

	METRIC	IMPERIAL	AMERICAN
Carrots, sliced diagonally	450 g	I lb	I lb
Parsnips, sliced	450 g	I lb	I lb
Clear honey	30 ml	2 tbsp	2 tbsp
Butter or margarine	75 g	3 oz	⅓ cup
Onion, chopped	I	I	I
Water	300 ml	½ pt	I ¼ cups
Fresh mint leaves, chopped	3	3	3
Salt and freshly ground black pepper			

① Place all the ingredients except the seasoning in a casserole (Dutch oven).

② Cover and cook in a preheated oven at 180°C/350°F/gas mark 4 for 1 hour until the liquid has almost evaporated.

③ Season to taste with salt and pepper before serving.

PREPARATION TIME: 10 MINUTES
COOKING TIME: 1 HOUR

NEPAL-STYLE CAULIFLOWER

Soaking cauliflower in an acid such as vinegar or lemon juice makes the finished dish crisp. Before cooking, cut off the outer leaves and the main core. There is no need to remove the inner tender green leaves. Use Madras curry powder instead of saffron powder if you prefer a stronger flavour.

—— SERVES 4 ——

	METRIC	IMPERIAL	AMERICAN
Cauliflower	I	I	I
Juice and grated rind of I lemon			
Water	300 ml	½ pt	1¼ cups
Salt and freshly ground black pepper			
Mild mustard	5 ml	I tsp	I tsp
Clear honey	5 ml	I tsp	I tsp
Saffron powder	5 ml	I tsp	I tsp
Plain yoghurt	120 ml	4 fl oz	½ cup
Chopped fresh coriander (cilantro)	30 ml	2 tbsp	2 tbsp

① Divide the cauliflower into florets and soak them in the lemon juice with the grated rind for 1 hour. Drain.

② Place the cauliflower and water in a casserole (Dutch oven) and season to taste with salt and pepper.

③ Cook, uncovered, in a preheated oven at 180°C/350°F/gas mark 4 for 30 minutes.

④ Mix together the mustard, honey, saffron powder and yoghurt and blend into the cauliflower liquid. Cook for a further 5–10 minutes.

⑤ Sprinkle the coriander over the cauliflower florets and serve.

PREPARATION TIME: 15 MINUTES
COOKING TIME: 40 MINUTES

BRAISED BUTTERED CELERY

This French recipe is often served as an accompaniment to roast pheasant or guinea fowl, but it is equally delicious on its own.

—— SERVES 4 ——

	METRIC	IMPERIAL	AMERICAN
Small heads of celery	2	2	2
Butter or margarine	25 g	1 oz	2 tbsp
Chicken or veal stock	600 ml	1 pt	2½ cups
Salt and freshly ground black pepper			
Cheddar cheese, grated	150 g	5 oz	1¼ cups
Chopped fresh parsley	30 ml	2 tbsp	2 tbsp

1. Trim the root off each head of celery. Wash and scrub under cold running water. Par-boil them for 10 minutes, then drain and cut each head in half.

2. Melt the butter or margarine in a flameproof casserole (Dutch oven), arrange the celery on top and cover with the stock. Season to taste with salt and pepper.

3. Cover and braise in a preheated oven at 180°C/350°F/gas mark 4 for 1 hour.

4. Sprinkle over the grated cheese and parsley and serve with a trickle of the reduced stock.

PREPARATION TIME: 15 MINUTES
COOKING TIME: 1 HOUR

MEXICAN SWEETCORN CASSEROLE WITH CHILLI

Add a little more stock and you can serve this recipe as Pancho Villa Soup.

—— SERVES 4 ——

	METRIC	IMPERIAL	AMERICAN
Cooked or canned sweetcorn (corn) kernels	450 g	1 lb	1 lb
Red (bell) pepper, seeded and diced	1	1	1
Onion, chopped	1	1	1
Cooked fresh or frozen peas	150 g	5 oz	5 oz
1 green chilli, seeded and chopped			
Chicken stock or water	600 ml	1 pt	2½ cups
Salt and freshly ground black pepper			
Avocado	1	1	1
Lemon juice	10 ml	2 tsp	2 tsp
Single (light) cream	100 ml	3½ fl oz	scant ½ cup

① Place all the ingredients except the avocado, lemon juice and cream in a casserole (Dutch oven).

② Cover and braise at 180°C/350°F/gas mark 4 for 1 hour. Drain away some of the surplus cooking liquid.

③ Stone (pit) and dice the avocado at the last moment and sprinkle it with lemon juice. Stir it into the casserole with the cream.

④ Check and adjust the seasoning before serving.

PREPARATION TIME: 10 MINUTES
COOKING TIME: 1 HOUR

INDIAN-STYLE POTATO CASSEROLE

This is one of my favourite potato dishes, a delicious meal in itself. Use new potatoes or the red-skinned, waxy kind that do not break up during cooking. To toast the coconut, toss in a dry pan over a gentle heat for a few minutes, until golden.

—— SERVES 4 ——

	METRIC	IMPERIAL	AMERICAN
New potatoes, scrubbed	450 g	I lb	I lb
Onion, chopped	I	I	I
Oil	60 ml	4 tbsp	4 tbsp
Curry powder	15 ml	I tbsp	I tbsp
Tomato purée (paste)	15ml	I tbsp	I tbsp
White cabbage, shredded or chopped	150 g	5 oz	5 oz
Water	600 ml	I pt	2½ cups
Garlic clove, chopped	I	I	I
Cooked fresh or frozen peas	100 g	4 oz	4 oz
Salt and freshly ground black pepper			
Desiccated (shredded) coconut, toasted	30 ml	2 tbsp	2 tbsp

① Place all the ingredients except the coconut in a casserole (Dutch oven).

② Cover and braise in a preheated oven at 180°C/350°F/gas mark 4 for 45 minutes until tender.

③ Drain away some of the juice or use it as gravy.

④ Sprinkle with the toasted coconut, then serve.

PREPARATION TIME: 10 MINUTES
COOKING TIME: 45 MINUTES

LATIN AMERICAN GUMBO CASSEROLE

Okra (ladies' fingers) are now available in most supermarkets. They are nutritious and very gelatinous and are one of the most popular vegetables in Indian cookery.

—— SERVES 4 ——

	METRIC	IMPERIAL	AMERICAN
Okra	450 g	1 lb	1 lb
Oil	45 ml	3 tbsp	3 tbsp
Onion, chopped	1	1	1
Tomatoes, skinned, seeded and chopped	3	3	3
Garlic cloves, chopped	3	3	3
Curry powder	15 ml	1 tbsp	1 tbsp
Green chilli, seeded and chopped	1	1	1
Salt			
Water	300 ml	½ pt	1¼ cups
Hard cheese, grated, or peanuts, chopped, to garnish	100 g	4 oz	1 cup

① Remove the stalks from the okra without bursting the pods. Place all the ingredients except the cheese or peanuts in a casserole (Dutch oven).

② Cover and braise in a preheated oven at 200°C/400°F/gas mark 6 for 30 minutes until tender.

③ Season with salt and sprinkle over the cheese or peanuts before serving.

PREPARATION TIME: 10 MINUTES
COOKING TIME: 30 MINUTES

WELSH-STYLE LEEK CASSEROLE

Young leeks are best for this casserole so that both the white and green parts can be used. To remove any dirt in the leeks, cut a zig-zag line down the centre to open up the leek so that the dirt can be washed out under running water.

—— SERVES 4 ——

	METRIC	IMPERIAL	AMERICAN
Small leeks, cleaned	8	8	8
Slices of ham	4	4	4
Chicken stock	300 ml	½ pt	1¼ cups
Dry sherry	100 ml	3½ fl oz	scant ½ cup
Salt and freshly ground black pepper			
Cheddar cheese, grated	100 g	4 oz	1 cup

① Layer the leeks and ham in a casserole (Dutch oven), cover with the stock and sherry and season to taste with salt and pepper.

② Cover and braise in a preheated oven at 200°C/400°F/gas mark 6 for 35 minutes until the vegetables are tender.

③ Drain off the surplus liquid and sprinkle over the grated cheese before serving.

PREPARATION TIME: 5 MINUTES
COOKING TIME: 35 MINUTES

PUMPKIN CASSEROLE WITH GINGER
—— SERVES 4 ——

	METRIC	IMPERIAL	AMERICAN
Pumpkin, peeled, seeded and cubed	450 g	1 lb	1 lb
Onion, chopped	1	1	1
Piece of fresh root ginger, peeled and chopped	2.5 cm	1 in	1 in
Lean bacon rashers (slices), rinded and diced	4	4	4
Chicken stock or water	600 ml	1 pt	2½ cups
Butter or margarine	50 g	2 oz	¼ cup
Salt and freshly ground black pepper			

① Combine all the ingredients in a casserole (Dutch oven).

② Cover and cook in a preheated oven at 200°C/400°F/gas mark 6 for 30 minutes until tender.

③ Drain off the surplus liquid and serve.

PREPARATION TIME: 15 MINUTES
COOKING TIME: 30 MINUTES

SWEET AND SOUR ONIONS WITH SULTANAS

This dish makes a delicious starter or side dish and works best with even-sized onions.

—— SERVES 4 ——

	METRIC	IMPERIAL	AMERICAN
Small onions or shallots	16	16	16
White wine vinegar	50 ml	2 fl oz	3½ tbsp
Clear honey	45 ml	3 tbsp	3 tbsp
Sugar	50 g	2 oz	¼ cup
Sweet white wine	100 ml	3½ fl oz	scant ½ cup
Anise seeds	5 ml	1 tsp	1 tsp
Sultanas (golden raisins)	50 g	2 oz	⅓ cup
Water	100 ml	3½ fl oz	scant ½ cup
Salt and freshly ground black pepper			

① Place all the ingredients in a shallow casserole (Dutch oven).

② Cover and braise in a preheated oven at 180°C/350°F/gas mark 4 for 45 minutes until the liquid has evaporated, checking every 10 minutes. If necessary, cook for a little longer to reduce the liquid.

③ Serve cold as an hors d'oeuvre or as an accompaniment for cold meat.

PREPARATION TIME: 15 MINUTES
COOKING TIME: 45 MINUTES

FRENCH-STYLE BABY PEAS

This dish was famous at the time of Louis XIV and tastes just as good now, served on its own or as an accompaniment for duck. Choose tiny onions, no bigger than grapes.

—— SERVES 4 ——

	METRIC	IMPERIAL	AMERICAN
Lettuce heart, shredded	I	I	I
Shelled fresh baby peas	450 g	I lb	I lb
Button (pearl) onions	12	12	12
Butter or margarine	100 g	4 oz	½ cup
Water	120 ml	4 fl oz	½ cup
Salt and freshly ground black pepper			
Sugar	5 ml	I tsp	I tsp
Cornflour (cornstarch)	5 ml	I tsp	I tsp

① Place all ingredients except the cornflour in a flameproof casserole (Dutch oven).

② Cover and braise in a preheated oven at 180°C/350°F/gas mark 4 for 30 minutes.

③ Blend the cornflour with a little water, then stir it into the casserole. Bring to the boil on top of the stove and simmer for a few minutes until thickened, stirring continuously.

PREPARATION TIME: 10 MINUTES
COOKING TIME: 30 MINUTES

GREEN LENTILS WITH HAZELNUTS

This nourishing dish can be served as a main-course dish.

—— SERVES 4 ——

	METRIC	IMPERIAL	AMERICAN
Green lentils, soaked in cold water for 2 hours	150 g	5 oz	scant I cup
Hazelnuts (filberts)	150 g	5 oz	1¼ cups
Small onions	150 g	5 oz	5 oz
Tomatoes, skinned, seeded and chopped	2	2	2
Yeast extract	15 ml	I tbsp	I tbsp
Water	600 ml	I pt	2½ cups
Salt and freshly ground black pepper			
Butter or margarine	50 g	2 oz	¼ cup
French dressing or boiled rice, to serve			

① Place all the ingredients in a casserole (Dutch oven).

② Cover and braise in a preheated oven at 180°C/350°F/gas mark 4 for 40 minutes until all the ingredients are tender.

③ Pour away any excess liquid and serve cold with a French dressing or hot with boiled rice.

PREPARATION TIME: 10 MINUTES PLUS SOAKING
COOKING TIME: 40 MINUTES

FRUIT CASSEROLES

Many types of fresh and dried fruits gain extra flavour when poached in a syrup. The addition of spices such as cinnamon, cloves, aniseed, mint and lemon grass gives a special fragrance. The fragile texture of many fruits requires very slow cooking to allow the syrup to permeate the flesh of the fruit, while preventing the skin from splitting and the flesh from disintegrating.

The compôtes in this chapter can be served alone, or with ice cream or set custards. With certain syrups, I recommend that a tea bag be added towards the end of the cooking time to give a tang to the syrup.

ORIENTAL FIG CASSEROLE

There are over 600 species of fig grown in the world and, being the sweetest of the fruits, they can be cooked with only a small amount of added sugar.

—— SERVES 4 ——

	METRIC	IMPERIAL	AMERICAN
Fresh red figs	1 kg	2¼ lb	2¼ lb
Fresh raspberries	150 g	5 oz	¾ cup
Caster (superfine) sugar	150 g	5 oz	¾ cup
Cinnamon stick	1	1	1
Slices of lemon	4	4	4
Red wine	150 ml	¼ pt	⅔ cup
Water	300 ml	½ pt	1¼ cups
Rice or semolina (cream of wheat) pudding or almond biscuits (cookies), to serve			

① Wash and pat the figs dry. Place in a casserole (Dutch oven) with the other ingredients.

② Cook in a preheated oven at 180°C/350°F/gas mark 4 for 30 minutes.

③ Serve with rice or semolina pudding or almond biscuits.

PREPARATION TIME: 5 MINUTES
COOKING TIME: 30 MINUTES

PEAR COMPÔTE

Pears, which are native to Europe and Western Asia, have been cultivated since earliest times. They may be cooked when they are still firm and not completely ripe. For flavour, it is best to use ripe pears with the peel added as a separate flavour enhancer. William, Conference or Comice are the best varieties.

—— SERVES 4 ——

	METRIC	IMPERIAL	AMERICAN
Comice pears, peeled, cored and halved	4	4	4
Water	300 ml	½ pt	1¼ cups
Caster (superfine) sugar	150 g	5 oz	¾ cup
Cloves	4	4	4
Anise seeds	5 ml	1 tsp	1 tsp
Tea bag	1	1	1
Anisette liqueur (optional)	15 ml	1 tbsp	1 tbsp

① Place the pear peel and seeds in a flameproof casserole (Dutch oven) with the water, sugar, cloves and anise seeds, if using. Arrange the pears on top. Bring to the boil, then cover and simmer gently for 30 minutes until soft.

② Remove from the heat, add the tea bag, cover and leave to stand for 8 minutes.

③ Transfer the pears to a warm serving dish and sprinkle with the anisette liqueur, if using. Discard the tea bag and strain the syrup to serve separately.

PREPARATION TIME: 10 MINUTES
COOKING TIME: 30 MINUTES PLUS STANDING

PEACHES AND NECTARINES IN BLACKCURRANT

Peaches should be peeled for cooked desserts, but nectarines may be served with the skin on.

—— SERVES 4 ——

	METRIC	IMPERIAL	AMERICAN
Peaches	4	4	4
Nectarines	4	4	4
Blackcurrant cordial	30 ml	2 tbsp	2 tbsp
Granulated sugar	150 g	5 oz	¾ cup
Water	300 ml	½ pt	1¼ cups
Brandy or gin	45 ml	3 tbsp	3 tbsp
Ice cream, to serve			

① Scald the peaches in boiling water for 1–2 minutes, then immerse them in cold water. Peel the skins downwards in strips, using a small knife. Cut the peaches in half and remove the stones (pits). Leave the nectarines whole.

② Place the peaches and nectarines in a casserole (Dutch oven) and add the cordial, sugar and water.

③ Poach in a preheated oven at 180°C/350°F/gas mark 4 for 15 minutes.

④ Leave to cool in the syrup, then add the brandy or gin and serve with ice cream.

PREPARATION TIME: 5 MINUTES
COOKING TIME: 15 MINUTES

APPLE CASSEROLE

Eating (dessert) apples are best used for compôtes as they do not disintegrate during cooking. The best varieties are Cox's Orange Pippin, Orleans Reinette and Egremont Russet.

—— SERVES 4 ——

	METRIC	IMPERIAL	AMERICAN
Eating (dessert) apples, peeled and cored	8	8	8
Apple juice	300 ml	½ pt	1¼ cups
Light brown sugar	50 g	5 oz	¾ cup
Juice of I lemon			
Cinnamon stick	I	I	I
Soured (dairy sour) cream or plain yoghurt, to serve			

① Place all the ingredients in a casserole (Dutch oven).

② Cover and cook in a preheated oven at 180°C/350°F/gas mark 4 for 20 minutes.

③ Leave to cool, then serve with soured cream or yoghurt.

PREPARATION TIME: 5 MINUTES
COOKING TIME: 20 MINUTES

PRUNES IN RED WINE

—— SERVES 4 ——

	METRIC	IMPERIAL	AMERICAN
Californian prunes, stoned (pitted)	I kg	I lb	I lb
Red wine	300 ml	½ pt	1¼ cups
Ground cinnamon	5 ml	I tsp	I tsp
A pinch of grated nutmeg			
A pinch of ground cloves			
Slices of lemon	4	4	4
Rice pudding, blancmange or shortbread (shortcake), to serve			

①   Soak the prunes in the wine with the spices and lemon for 3 hours until swollen. Place in a casserole (Dutch oven).

②   Cook in a preheated oven at 180°C/350°F/gas mark 4 for 20 minutes. Remove the lemon.

③   Leave to cool, then serve with rice pudding, blancmange or shortbread.

PREPARATION TIME: 2 MINUTES PLUS SOAKING
COOKING TIME: 20 MINUTES

APRICOT CASSEROLE IN LIME CORDIAL

This is my favourite way of cooking apricots, which should not be overcooked or they tend to get mushy. Halve and stone (pit) the fruit if you prefer – but I think they are best left whole.

—— SERVES 4 ——

	METRIC	IMPERIAL	AMERICAN
Freshly brewed Ceylon tea	300 ml	½ pt	1¼ cups
Fresh apricots, firm and not too ripe	1 kg	2¼ lb	2¼ lb
Lime cordial	100 ml	3½ fl oz	scant ½ cup
Granulated sugar	100 g	4 oz	½ cup
Kirsch (optional)	30 ml	2 tbsp	2 tbsp
Cream, ice cream or rice pudding, to serve			

①   Strain the tea into a casserole (Dutch oven). Add the apricots, lime cordial and sugar.

②   Cover and poach in a preheated oven at 180°C/350°F/gas mark 4 for 6 minutes.

③   Leave to cool in the syrup, then stir in the kirsch, if using, before serving with cream, ice cream or rice pudding.

PREPARATION TIME: 10 MINUTES
COOKING TIME: 6 MINUTES

WINTER FRUIT COMPÔTE

In the winter, a mixture of dried fruits such as apples, prunes, pears, raisins, apricots and peaches can be enjoyed in a compôte. To maximise the flavour, these fruits should be soaked in freshly brewed tea until swollen.

—— SERVES 4 ——

	METRIC	IMPERIAL	AMERICAN
Assorted dried fruits	450 g	1 lb	1 lb
Freshly brewed tea, strained	600 ml	1 pt	2½ cups
Clear honey	45 ml	3 tbsp	3 tbsp
Light brown sugar	100 g	4 oz	½ cup
Ground cinnamon	5 ml	1 tsp	1 tsp
Juice of 1 lemon			
Ice cream or hot custard, to serve			

① Place the fruit in a casserole (Dutch oven), pour in the strained tea and leave to soak for 3 hours.

② Stir in the honey and cinnamon.

③ Cook in a preheated oven at 180°C/350°F/gas mark 4 for 30 minutes.

④ Leave to cool, then chill overnight.

⑤ Add the lemon juice before serving with ice cream or hot custard.

PREPARATION TIME: 5 MINUTES PLUS SOAKING
COOKING TIME: 30 MINUTES

RHUBARB AND STRAWBERRY COMPÔTE

There can be no better combination for flavour and refreshing taste than tender, pink rhubarb with soft fruits, such as strawberries. The addition of ginger, too, can make a big difference. Main-crop rhubarb is fibrous and has to be scraped well all over. The best way to cook it to prevent pulping is in a casserole (Dutch oven) with a heavy syrup, which will hold the fruit together firmly.

—— SERVES 4 ——

	METRIC	IMPERIAL	AMERICAN
Fresh young rhubarb, cut into 3 cm/1¼ in pieces	450 g	1 lb	1 lb
Fresh strawberries	150 g	5 oz	¾ cup
Piece of fresh root ginger, grated	2.5 cm	1 in	1 in
Red or rosé wine	150 ml	¼ pt	⅔ cup
Granulated sugar	225 g	8 oz	1 cup
Powdered gelatine	25 g	1 oz	1 sachet
A few drops of red food colouring (optional)			
Custard or ice cream, to serve			

①　Place the fruit in a casserole (Dutch oven) with the ginger and wine.

②　Mix the sugar and gelatine, add the food colouring, if using, and sprinkle this mixture over the fruits.

③　Cover and cook in a preheated oven at 180°C/350°F/gas mark 4 for 8 minutes.

④　Leave to cool, then chill before serving with custard or ice cream.

PREPARATION TIME: 10 MINUTES
COOKING TIME: 8 MINUTES

JAMAICAN BUTTERSCOTCH BANANAS

Bananas have their best flavour when they are eaten either very ripe or baked in a casserole (Dutch oven). My favourite recipe, which I brought back from Jamaica, cooks them with butter, sugar and rum.

—— SERVES 4 ——

	METRIC	IMPERIAL	AMERICAN
Bananas, not too ripe	8	8	8
Caster (superfine) sugar	100 g	4 oz	½ cup
Unsalted butter	100 g	4 oz	½ cup
Juice of 1 orange			
Jamaican rum	15 ml	1 tbsp	1 tbsp
Chocolate or coffee ice cream, to serve			

① Peel the bananas and place them in a casserole with the sugar, butter, orange juice and rum.

② Bake in a preheated oven at 180°C/350°F/gas mark 4 for 10 minutes until the butter turns into a creamy and sticky butterscotch.

③ Leave to cool before serving with chocolate or coffee ice cream.

PREPARATION TIME: 5 MINUTES
COOKING TIME: 10 MINUTES

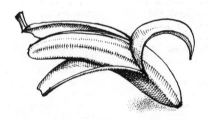

INDEX